Success in College

Using the Internet

Jack Pejsa
Winona State University

Success in College

Using the Internet

Jack Pejsa
Winona State University

Houghton Mifflin Company   Boston   New York

Associate Editor: Melissa Plumb

Project Editor: Elizabeth Gale Napolitano

Production/Design Coordinator: Jennifer Meyer

Senior Manufacturing Coordinator: Florence Cadran

Editorial Assistant: Christian Zabriskie

Printed in the U.S.A.

Library of Congress Catalog Card Number: 97-72532

ISBN: 0-395-83016-8

123456789-SB-01-00-99-98-97

This book is dedicated to my mother,
Jeanne Hill Pejsa
1927–1995

Contents

Preface

As we peer around the corner into the twenty-first century, one measure of success for students is their ability to effectively use the vast resources available at their fingertips on the Internet. As they make their way through college and move into the world of work, students will need to know what the Internet is, how it works, and how they can best use it. *Success in College Using the Internet* can help students begin this process.

I have written *Success in College Using the Internet* for college students who want to learn about the Internet and how they can navigate it. It is not intended to answer every question students might have about the Internet; rather, it is meant for students who wish to find Internet resources and supplements to their educational experience. The text focuses on making it as easy as possible for students to use the Internet as a communication and research tool.

Navigating the World Wide Web

From the beginning I have envisioned this book as a supportive text in a hands-on learning environment. I firmly believe that the most effective way for students to learn about the Internet is to get online and work hand-in-hand with both a competent tutor and an instructional guide. This textbook and its accompanying Web site are that tutor and that guide.

In Print and Online   Screen shots of Web sites are included throughout the text to give students an accurate feel for the nature of the Internet resources under discussion. However, because changes occur so rapidly in this medium, a Web site address that is current and active one day may well have disappeared or changed the next. To deal with the variable nature of Internet resource links and changing site addresses, the idea of creating a Web site and integrating it with the text was born. The *Success in College Using the Internet* Web site can be found at

http://www.luminet.net/~jackp/success.htm

Students who have access to the Web and even minimal browser skills can log on to the site and surf along as we explore the breadth and depth of Web resources. The first page of the site includes a list of "Links to Sites Illustrated in the Text." Students can reach most of the sites shown in the text by selecting the appropriate figure number and caption from this list.

Expanding the Journey   The Web site will be updated frequently as the Internet changes and grows. The following features will be added to it over time:

- **An online glossary** will include key words used in the text, with a link to a computer glossary Web site.

- Links to **additional readings** will provide students with alternate or additional explanations of the various topics discussed in each chapter.

- **Extended Internet exercises** will increase the number and breadth of sites that are discussed. Over time, I will seek out the very best emerging sites for students, highlight them on the site, and provide exercises related to the sites.

Experiencing Success in College Using the Internet

Success in College Using the Internet will help you show your students just how valuable the Internet can be. I present topics and concepts gradually to avoid overwhelming students and to allow them to master elementary skills before working on more complex skills. However, each chapter can be read relatively independently of the others, so you can skip chapters or rearrange the order of chapters as your students' needs dictate. Chapter 3, for example, discusses the fundamentals of the Internet at a deeper level than may be necessary for students in some courses. It can be bypassed with no significant loss of continuity. In addition, students can read any chapters that you do not cover in class on their own.

After reading this text, whether for your course or independently, students will:

> ***Understand just what the Internet is and how it works.***   Chapters 1 and 3 provide a thorough overview of the Internet. I also answer questions students may have, such as "Is the Internet difficult to master?", "Why should *I* use the Internet?", and "How can I use the Internet in my classes or research projects?".

> ***Know how to make the Internet work for them.***   *Success in College Using the Internet* answers in depth just why students should use the Internet. I begin by discussing e-mail in Chapter 2, and the World Wide Web in Chapter 4, and move on to the more advanced and in-depth topics and applications, such as newsgroups in Chapter 5, and other resource sites on the Internet, such as telnet and gopher in Chapter 6.

Feel more confident about navigating the Internet. Many of the exercises in the book ask students to do what I firmly believe is necessary for them to feel comfortable with the Internet: get online and explore the wealth of valuable resources available. Students are asked to visit their computer center, share e-mail messages with classmates, subscribe to discussion lists, find sites on the World Wide Web that will be helpful to them (and bookmark them), research online libraries using telnet, visit newsgroups appropriate to their areas of interest and study, and much more.

Grasp the technicalities of the Internet more easily—or know where to find the answers. Review questions in each chapter reinforce information students learn in class and from the book. The questions are based on the what, why, where, and how of the Internet skills taught in the chapter.

Know how to use Web search engines and virtual libraries. Throughout *Success in College Using the Internet*, I emphasize the use of search engines and comprehensive subject indices known as virtual libraries. This built-in anti-obsolescence feature shows students that, although specific sites may change and grow, search engines and virtual libraries can always help them find the newest and most up-to-date links on the Internet.

Acknowledgments

I want to thank the following people at Houghton Mifflin Company who supported this endeavor: Barbara Heinssen, Director of Student Success Programs; Melissa Plumb; and Bill Webber. I would also like to thank my literary agent, Robert Lieberman; Monica Freking for her endless emotional support during the course of the project; Terri Burrell for her encouragement as well as her financial assistance; my brother, Jim Pejsa, for introducing me to the Internet; and my sister, Anita Johnston, and my father, Art Pejsa, and his wife, Jane, who provided financial support at the early stages of the development of this book.

I also want to thank the Hiawatha Foundation and *Luminet* in Winona, Minnesota, who continue to provide ongoing support for the development of this project, including Internet access privileges and server space for the Web site that accompanies the text.

Finally, I want to thank all the reviewers who helped me create this book:

Sharon Gagel, University of North Carolina—Charlotte

Irene Honey, University of Colorado

Charles D. Horn, Broward Community College (FL)

Nancy Mathias, St. Norbert College (WI)

Chris Miller, Hartwick College (NY)

Nancy L. Stegall, DeVry Institute of Technology—Phoenix

Ellen Taricani, Pennsylvania State University

Barbara Wade, Pennsylvania State University

I welcome your feedback. As you move through *Success in College Using the Internet* and its accompanying Web site, e-mail me (jackp@luminet.net) your suggestions and thoughts on ways to improve the book.

J. P.

Chapter 1

Welcome to the Internet

1.1 Overview

In this first chapter, we will present an overview of the Internet: what it is, where it came from, who uses it, some resources and tools which are useful for students, and a list of some fairly compelling reasons for students to learn to use the power of this worldwide electronic information network for achieving success in their academic endeavors.

1.2 What Is the Internet?

The Internet is an exceptionally large computer *network* which spans a large part of the world we live in, and which has a number of tremendously powerful capabilities for sharing and communicating information between the people (users) of this network, through their computers.

Technically speaking, all computers that are "connected" to the Internet have the capability of sharing information and communications with each other. In many ways, the Internet works in a similar way to the telephone system we are all familiar with and use every day. People who have telephones in their homes or places of business and are connected to their local telephone company's network have the capability of communicating with other people who also have telephones, on a local basis as well as nationwide and even across the world at large (through the use of long-distance and overseas telephone networks).

Sending a fax, for example, over the telephone line, whether it be to a business down the street or to an individual half a world away, is a relatively simple process (from the telephone user's point of view). One only needs to know the telephone number of the party who will be the recipient of the fax, turn on the fax machine, make the connection, insert the document to be faxed into the machine, and the job is finished!

Information transmitted over the Internet works in a very similar fashion: documents are shared on this world network by first converting them into a form that can be stored on computers (unless they're already in that form), connecting the computer to the Internet, establishing a connection with the receiving party or with an intermediate party (such as a "mail server" computer), and sending the document to its destination using one of the Internet tools designed for that purpose, such as *electronic mail* (e-mail) or *file transfer protocol* (FTP). E-mail and FTP are discussed in detail in later chapters of this text.

Speaking again from a technical point of view, information shared and communicated via the Internet pathways is always first converted from its original form into "electronic" form, which means it is translated into *"bits"* and *"bytes"* of electrical information the computer can understand and process. Once it has been converted into electronic form, computers have exceptionally powerful capabilities for storing, compressing, and transmitting such information to other computers on the Internet in an extremely efficient and reliable manner.

This text will not concern itself with the details of how all this technology works. Instead, it will focus on how the student can *use* the Internet for finding resources of value, and for utilizing its considerable communications and information retrieval capabilities for educational purposes.

1.3   A Brief History of the Internet

What we know today as the Internet began in the late 1960s as an academic research network, which was used primarily by scientists, engineers, and other technical professionals as a means of sharing scientific information and exchanging electronic-based communications between each other through their respective computer systems.

An early form of what is now the Internet was known as ARPANET (the Advanced Research Projects Agency Network), which, by the early 1970s, had connected computer facilities of over 50 universities and research centers across the United States. Much of the early research and development on ARPANET was for military and defense purposes, which resulted in the design and engineering of a network that was highly reliable and relatively secure against breakdowns due to network failures.

During the late 1970s and 1980s, other computer networks came into widespread existence with names like UUCP (which connected computers using the Unix operating system), CSNET (Computer Science Network), Bitnet, CERFnet, and Usenet. All or parts of these networks changed in form, or died away entirely, as the technological world evolved and developed, and then these various smaller networks merged to form the large world-encompassing network we now call the Internet.

Although many of the early ground-breaking efforts in the development of computer networks were for scientific, engineering, research, and military purposes, the Internet world of today has a much broader spectrum of users and applications. College students, for example, use the Internet for a wide variety of educational purposes (which is the subject of this book), including having immediate access to a voluminous breadth of up-to-date information on an almost limitless variety of topics, and for electronic-based communications between other students, faculty members, and researchers.

1.4   Who Uses the Internet?

Although the Internet was originally developed as a scientific and research information sharing network, its users now include people of all ages and backgrounds, many of whom have little or no scientific or technical interests or training whatsoever.

Students using the Internet do not need to be computer "freaks" or otherwise engage an interest in the technology behind the Internet, any more than it is necessary for people using a telephone or fax machine to be schooled in electronic communications technology. Principally, the Internet has evolved into becoming a universal *information-sharing tool*. It is usable by virtually anyone who has minimal computer literacy and a handful of skills necessary to effectively use the basic tools of Internet communications and information retrieval. In addition, users need a connection to the Internet, which links the computer being used at their local site to this worldwide network.

In addition to students, researchers, and faculty members at colleges and universities, teachers at all levels are becoming Internet literate in very large numbers due to its potentially positive applications in education for learners of all ages and backgrounds. Current Internet student users include individuals in ages ranging from the youngest schoolchildren who connect in their elementary school classrooms, or from their home computers through modems, to senior citizens who use a wide variety of the Internet's resources, including e-mail, newsgroups, and the *World Wide Web*.

Organizations and businesses, from the smallest in size to very large *Fortune 500* corporations, are utilizing the Internet for a large variety of purposes, including intracompany communications as well as outside communication with clients and customers. They also distribute a large variety of information about their enterprises to interested individuals throughout the world.

Also, many "ordinary" people now have Internet accounts and log on frequently to use electronic mail (e-mail) facilities and to "surf" the near-infinite range and diversity of resources distributed throughout the thousands of computer *servers* which constitute the network threads of the rapidly growing, powerful, and exceptionally popular World Wide Web (often called the "Web" for short). These trends are expected to continue in the near to distant future as many more communications and information resources are made available on the Internet, and an ever-increasing array of more powerful and easy-to-use tools are developed and become available to access these resources.

1.5   Is the Internet Difficult to Master?

In reality, the tools needed to access the power of the Internet's information resources and communication facilities are exceptionally easy to use and take very little time and few computer skills to master. Sending e-mail, for example, is a simple matter of starting the mail program on your computer, typing the *address* of the recipient of your message, inserting a *subject line* describing the nature of your message, entering the contents of the message itself, and sending it on its way with a mouse click or the press of a keystroke. Unlike a postal letter, you don't need to lick any stamps, address envelopes, look up ZIP codes, or drive (through rush-hour traffic) to the nearest post office (after you realize you've missed the deadline for the mailbox pickup at the corner).

Browsers, which are used by millions to navigate the World Wide Web (among other Internet resources), are so simple to use that they can be utilized by most students with less than an hour of training. Quickly branching from one document to another on the Internet is as simple as clicking the mouse on a *hot link* on the viewing screen, which is simply a highlighted area (displayed in a different color or typeface) that enables a quick and rapid connection to a related Web document located elsewhere on the Internet (Web).

1.6   How to Gain Access to the Internet

Essentially, what is needed to access the Internet is a computer which has been "connected" through a *local-area network* (LAN), such as a PC or Macintosh network in a campus computer lab, media center, or library. Alternatively, a student may directly connect from home or a residence hall through a *modem* (which connects the computer to the Internet via the telephone line). Additionally, some extra *software* (and sometimes *hardware*, such as a circuit board in the computer) may need to be installed to complete the connection. Furthermore, the student needs to have a *user account* with an *Internet service provider* (ISP) or with the computer system on campus. An account gives the student "access privileges" to use the computer for the purpose of connecting to other computers locally, and to other computers worldwide through the Internet.

1.7   Internet Resources for Education

The Internet has a voluminous collection and variety of information and communication resources which are easily accessible by students who have the skills to access and use this powerful information medium. In addition, the Internet is an exceptionally powerful communications network, and a large body of current network traffic is the exchange of communications in the form of electronic mail messages between Internet users. Various excellent tools on the Internet of great value to students are detailed in the remaining chapters of this book.

1.8   Tools for Communication

An exceptionally widespread use of the Internet is as a tool for electronic communications between individuals who are connected to each other by this medium. Although it is not the only means for exchanging messages between individuals on the Internet, e-mail is certainly a most important and prolific application of this worldwide communications network.

Another important use of the Internet is for communicating publicly on the "electronic bulletin boards" called *newsgroups.* Messages can be easily placed by students to a newsgroup where they may (possibly) be read by many tens of thousands of interested persons worldwide. Newsgroups can be an excellent resource for discussions and the exchange of information between individuals who maintain common interests in particular subjects or areas of knowledge.

The *World Wide Web* (WWW) has been growing in popularity by leaps and bounds in recent years, and one of the reasons for its tremendous growth has been its exceptional ease of use. Existing in ever-increasing abundance are "chat rooms" where individuals can exchange ideas and thoughts with other Internet users in "real time." For example, during the 1996 Super Bowl, a Web page chat room was visited by tens of thousands of sports enthusiasts who discussed their opinions about the game *while it was in progress.*

Internet Relay Chat (IRC) also allows students to communicate with each other over the Internet in a real-time "conversational" mode. IRC has the potential to be effectively utilized as an educational medium. For example, online study sessions could be easily conducted over IRC, allowing students worldwide to ask questions, review topics, and talk over issues about a specific course or subject.

1.9   Tools for Information Gathering and Research

The second most important use of the Internet is as a means of information gathering and research purposes. It may be helpful to think of the Internet as a worldwide, gigantic *virtual library* of resources, which are stored in electronic form and distributed throughout the world in thousands of computer-based "file cabinets." This huge distribution of information would not be so vitally important for students if it weren't for the fact that these resources are so *easily accessible* to anyone connected to the Internet. This enormous body of resources can be searched, browsed, printed, examined in detail, and even retrieved electronically by Internet users in an exceptionally short period of time, often in only a few seconds or minutes at the most.

1.10   Ten Applications of the Internet for Students

1.   **E-mail:** The advantages for the student gaining facility with e-mail communications over the Internet simply cannot be overstated. This communication tool is the primary (and most heavily used) application of the Internet, and literally millions of e-mail messages are exchanged between Internet users daily. It's a simple tool to learn, and sending an e-mail message through the Internet is as easy as mailing a postal letter: one only needs to address the e-mail to the recipient, type in the subject of the message (along with the content of the message) and send it on its way to its destination, where it will arrive in minutes (instead of the days it takes through the conventional postal system).

     For example, students can exchange e-mail with other students in their classes at the school they are attending, or with those at other educational institutions in other parts of the country or world. Further, they can use it to exchange communications with faculty and staff members at their college. (Many instructors currently use e-mail to distribute course materials, including syllabi, class and lecture notes, review and supplementary materials, student feedback, and even to conduct online quizzes and exams.)

     It is also possible for students writing term papers or conducting research to communicate directly via e-mail with researchers in their field of study. Many valuable professional contacts can be made in this fashion. In addition, students pursuing internships or employment opportunities can effectively use e-mail to directly contact representatives of companies or organizations they are exploring for this purpose.

     It's a very simple process for a student who has Internet access with an account to subscribe to free, e-mail-based newsletters, magazines, mailing lists, and *user groups* in their areas of interest or investigation. Politically inclined students may easily send letters to their congressmen or other representatives expressing their viewpoints on issues of concern. The applications of e-mail communications are formidable for the enterprising student, and this extremely popular form of communication via the Internet will be investigated in depth in the following chapter.

2.   **World Wide Web:** The Web is an outstanding mechanism for locating and browsing resources located throughout the world's great libraries, universities, and research institutions. There is no doubt that the Web is the most exciting recent development in Internet tools for users seeking information rapidly across a very large variety of disciplines and infor-

mation source types. The growth rate of organizations, educational institutions, research centers, businesses of all types, and *individuals* who are providing free information for distribution worldwide on the Web is simply astronomical. (For example, in 1994 the Web grew by a factor of 350,000%!)

As a student, you have the luxury of free access to all of this easy-to-locate and rapidly available information in an almost limitless range of subjects when you become a capable Internet user and have access to the tools required for Web browsing and information retrieval. Although not all Internet connections provide access to the Web, most educational institutions are providing those services and the tools (*Web browsers*) needed to access them because of the Web's exceptional importance and applicability for students and faculty engaged in learning and research.

Chapter 4 will explore a variety of resources available through the Web, including an online tour through a number of Web sites of particular usefulness to college students.

3. **Newsgroups:** These electronic bulletin boards of the Internet allow students to gain instant access to the most up-to-date news, information, resources, and communications from other Internet users worldwide. Many world experts in their fields regularly contribute to newsgroups in their specialty areas, and this information can be read by any individual with access to the Usenet network of newsgroups available through the Internet.

   Newsgroups are separated into logical categories and subcategories (and subsubcategories) in many thousands of areas of knowledge. Currently, well over 40,000 newsgroups are in existence on Usenet, and that number is expanding at an exceptional rate. Messages can be "posted" (and read by millions worldwide) on these newsgroup bulletin boards in a matter of minutes. Reading and contributing to Usenet newsgroups is the subject of Chapter 5 of this text.

4. **Telnet:** This Internet facility allows students to gain entry to a computer located at a distant location (even on the other side of the world) and use some of its capabilities as if they were local users sitting in the same room as the machine at the remote location. As an example, a student in Australia can connect through *telnet* to a large *supercomputer* at a research institution in the United States for the purpose of solving complex mathematical problems—which would be difficult or impossible

to solve on their "home" machine. Also, students can browse the enormous resources of the libraries at large universities and research institutions in search of books and periodicals of interest, and may (often) "download" information of interest to their local computer systems. Various educational applications of telnet are discussed in Chapter 6 of this text.

5. **FTP:** *File transfer protocol* is a means of accessing and retrieving a huge variety and breadth of freely available information, software, and other electronic resources from other computers over the Internet. *FTP* file transfers allow one server computer to make certain information and resources stored in its electronic file cabinets available to other users' "client" computers. Modern browsers, for navigating the Web, also come equipped with FTP capabilities so users of these tools can easily *search and retrieve* a voluminous body of information distributed throughout the world in the large network of FTP Internet server computers.

    The range of information and resources freely available via FTP facilities is simply enormous, and categories of documents accessible through this Internet facility include electronic books, journals, magazines, indexes, newspapers, computer reference manuals, software, music, poetry, graphics such as pictures, photographs, and art work, and a huge variety of other archived resources. Chapter 6 includes a section on the applications of FTP for college students and a set of online examples.

6. **WAIS:** *Wide-area information system* servers allow Internet users to search *databases* of information located in the libraries of universities and research institutions located throughout the world in a matter of minutes or less. Using *keyword searches*, student Internet users can scan millions of documents to find those which match the subject areas they wish to explore. Many college libraries allow WAIS searches of their holdings as an efficient mechanism for finding information of interest by students. Chapter 3 includes a section on using WAIS databases on the Internet for researching information in the large number of virtual libraries available worldwide.

7. **Cost:** For many student Internet users, there is no cost whatsoever to use the power and capabilities of the Internet through their campus computer networks. Since colleges and universities consider it of very high educational value to have this wide body of resources and communication capabilities available, many have acquired this technology to the significant

benefit of their students. In addition to four-year colleges and universities, many more community colleges, high schools, vocational and technical institutions, public libraries, and even elementary schools are connecting to the Internet in ever-rapidly expanding numbers.

8. **Reliability:** Unlike information stored on paper, there is a much greater *reliability* in communicating information in electronic form through the Internet, whether it be between computers located a few miles away or among those located on different sides of the earth! Electronic resources shared between users via the Internet "highways" are usually delivered with no loss of information along the way. Thanks to the engineering design of the Internet, it is capable of rapidly transmitting large volumes of information with a high degree of reliability. A student can feel relatively confident in sending a ten-thousand-word document through the Internet to a remote destination without the loss of even one character of information during the process!

9. **Speed of access:** Information can be transferred between computers on the Internet at an exceptionally high rate. The technology of electronic communications over this world computer network has improved so dramatically in recent years that resources can be accessed and retrieved, or communications can take place, in a matter of seconds or minutes that would have taken far greater amounts of time in the pre-Internet days. Using *Internet Relay Chat* (IRC), for example, a student can engage in a one-on-one conversation with another student located half a world away, in real time, while the delay in relaying sides of the conversation may be limited to seconds or less. Internet teleconferencing capabilities allow individuals to talk to each other as if using a telephone, though they may be located thousands of miles apart.

10. **It can be fun!** Using the Internet can be enjoyable for many students who are willing to take the time to learn minimal skills in using the tools to access it, and they gain the multitude of advantages it has to offer them. Unlike the many commands and skills necessary to effectively use the power of other computer application programs such as word processors, spreadsheets, desktop publishing programs, and database management systems, Internet software tools tend to be designed for less technically sophisticated users and are usually quite easy for most students to learn. Facility with a Web browser, for example, to access a gigantic volume of Internet resources, can be acquired to an acceptable degree in 15 minutes or less.

Summary

The Internet is a worldwide network of computers which is used for efficient and reliable information sharing and communications among individuals for a variety of purposes, including education and research. Developed as a scientific and defense research network approximately 30 years ago, its users now include people of all ages, cultures, and interests—a proportion of whom have minimal computer or technical backgrounds. Although the technology underlying the Internet is complex, the tools for accessing its tremendous capabilities are quite simple for students of all ages to use.

Accessing the Internet involves connecting the local computer through a network, or with a modem on a telephone line, to a larger system tied directly into the Internet. Sometimes additional computer hardware or software needs to be installed on the network or local machine to establish the connection. Also, a student must have a registered user account on the computer system to get online. At many educational institutions and in a variety of work environments, such accounts are provided free of charge to interested users. The primary and most popular use of the Internet is for e-mail correspondence with other users, which is a very convenient, rapid, and reliable form of worldwide electronic communications. FTP facilities allow Internet users to download resources from many information storage sites available on FTP server computers distributed worldwide. Telnet facilities allow remote access to a computer which could be thousands of miles away from the person who is using its capabilities. Libraries are a common example of information centers which allow telnet access to their resources. WAIS servers allow students the capability to efficiently search large databases of information on the computers distributed throughout the Internet. Newsgroups, the bulletin boards of the Internet, allow the free exchange of ideas and knowledge among millions of users worldwide. Newsgroups are divided into logical categories for easy access to relevant information of interest.

The advantages for the student in learning to use the Internet as an information-gathering and communications tool include its very low cost, ease of use, and the exceptional speed at which these resources can be browsed, searched, and retrieved (downloaded) to the student's local computer system. Information research and access or communicating through the Internet can be an enjoyable and educationally fruitful proposition for the student user once a minimal set of skills is developed and a bit of knowledge of the relevant Internet tools and online resources is acquired.

Review Questions

1. Describe two ways that students typically connect to the Internet.

2. Other than a computer, including hardware and software, what else must a student need for Internet access?

3. What are the two principal uses of the Internet?

4. Describe some uses of e-mail in the classroom.

5. What is the purpose of FTP facilities on the Internet?

6. Which Internet tool is used to search databases online?

7. Which Internet resource is expanding rapidly in popularity and uses a browser for access to its resources?

8. What is the purpose of a newsgroup, how many are currently in existence, and why are they broken into categories and subcategories?

9. Given the history of the development of the Internet, why do you suppose it has been engineered for exceptional information reliability?

10. Which Internet tool allows remote access to library computer systems?

Exercise

1. Pay a visit to the computer center at your college or educational institution. Write a descriptive summary of the following: the type of computer system in use, the number of computers connected to the network, whether or not Internet access is provided, what Internet tools are available for students to use, how one arranges to get an account on the system, and the number of student users currently accessing the Internet.

Chapter 2

E-mail: Worldwide Communications
for Students

2.1   Overview

Electronic mail (e-mail) is a form of worldwide electronic communications that is easy to use, very fast and reliable for exchanging messages with other individuals, and accessible by any student with an Internet e-mail account. There is a wide variety of useful applications of e-mail for college students. It is possible to send messages to more than one recipient at the same time, and "distribution lists" of members of a club or committee are easily constructed, greatly reducing the chore of sending e-mail to groups of individuals.

Files (documents) can be "attached" to e-mail messages, which makes it a simple task for students to easily and quickly share word processing documents, graphics, spreadsheet and database files, sounds or music, and computer programs. "Discussion lists" are a powerful use of Internet e-mail and allow a group of individuals to share regular communications on a topic of mutual interest. Many thousands of discussion lists currently exist, and subscribing to such lists is a very simple task, involving the sending of a single e-mail message to a "listserv" site on the Internet.

Although e-mail is the most widespread use of the Internet, other types of Internet-based communication include chat utilities, which allow individuals to carry on a conversation with each other in real time, and the Usenet newsgroups (discussed in the next chapter), for sharing information worldwide with people interested in related topics.

2.2   What Is E-mail?

It is a rare student who hasn't heard of electronic mail (or e-mail for short). E-mail is a means of conveniently, reliably, and *rapidly* communicating with

13

other students, professionals, and personal contacts on the local campus and throughout the world.

The use of electronic mail for communications includes the following advantages:

- **Speed**: E-mail reaches its destination quite quickly, relative to other means of communication, such as the postal system, often called "snail mail" by members of the Internet community. Most e-mail messages are delivered to their destination computers worldwide within a few hours (and often in much less time, depending on several factors related to the technology of the mail systems in use).

- **Reliability**: An e-mail message is nearly always delivered to the receiver *exactly* as it was sent—unless technical problems occur during transmission. The Internet was designed very carefully to attempt to ensure that information sent over its pathways is always transmitted and delivered in an exceptionally reliable way.

  Nevertheless, "glitches" do occur in the exchange of electronic mail between users of the Internet. Occasionally, an e-mail message you send may not successfully arrive at its destination, or vice versa. Unfortunately, as reliably as the Internet usually performs its services for users, the technology is not perfect. Network errors in message transmission may occur, computers can unexpectedly "go down," connections occasionally get broken, and various other mishaps are possible at any given time. (For example, in October of 1996, the Internet connection on the computer system of a major university campus was interrupted when dead rats were found on transmission wires in the system, resulting in a network breakdown!) Although the Internet technology is not without the possibility of malfunction, it remains an exceptionally reliable method for exchanging communications in the form of e-mail.

- **Accessibility**: It's easy to gain access and use e-mail facilities. Sending a message over the Internet, for example, is a relatively painless task for most students with an account on their campus computer system. It's often only a matter of walking to the closest computer lab, *logging on* to the Internet, starting the e-mail computer program in use, typing the text of the message onto the computer screen, and sending it along its way with the press of a key or two. A desirable feature of the Internet is its capability of exchanging mail messages among individuals at any hour of the day or night.

- **Range of coverage**: It is important to remember that e-mail is a worldwide communications system. Students can easily carry on regular correspondence with other students, friends, and colleagues on the Internet—regardless of their geographic location. Many students have maintained communications with researchers and professionals in their fields of study using e-mail facilities. E-mail can be a very fruitful means for discussing, exploring, and sharing research findings with other students and professionals.

- **Cost**: For a majority of students who have access to their campus computer system, there is no cost for connecting to the Internet and using its many facilities, including electronic mailing capabilities, for educational success. Many schools assign all students who will access the computer system an e-mail address for use on the local network, as well as through the Internet—allowing them the capability of sending and receiving mail with other students and Internet users throughout the world. Access to Internet e-mail then allows the student the many benefits of this most powerful means of communication.

- **Keeping records**: Since Internet messages are originated at a computer keyboard, and converted into electronic form, they can be easily saved for future reference. With most e-mailing systems, it is possible to maintain copies of all correspondence exchanged with others. This capability allows the student to keep an accurate record of messages sent and received through the Internet. Unlike the telephone or face-to-face communications, information exchanged through e-mail will not become garbled, distorted, or lost en route to its destination. Additionally, messages you send and receive through e-mail can be well "audited," as an accurate time and date stamping of your communications is included with each document sent. This can be a significant benefit when reviewing your correspondence at a later time. Also, mail can be maintained in separate electronic "file folders" on the computer for assisting you in organizing your mail for future reading or access.

- **Allows time to "compose" yourself**: Unlike a conversation on the telephone, composing and sending an e-mail message does not require you to collect and refine your thoughts all at once. You can prepare an e-mail message at your own leisure. Sometimes the information you have to share is incomplete, or you may need additional time to put it in the right words. There is no hurrying necessary when writing a document to be sent through e-mail. Usually your e-mail program will allow you to save your unfinished work before actually sending it through the Internet. Also, it is often possible to compose a message using a text editor or word processor on the computer system and later *copy and paste* it into your e-mail program when it is ready to be sent.

- **Send multiple copies at once**: Since e-mail is electronic correspondence, it can be easily manipulated by computers in a variety of useful ways. It is a simple matter for e-mail programs to generate *additional copies* of mail messages for sending duplicates to other intended recipients. A student sending mail can easily route an electronic *carbon copy* of a message to other individuals (or even to themselves for keeping as a record of the correspondence). *Distribution lists* are supported by many e-mail programs, allowing the capability of sending e-mail messages to many individuals at once. Students who work together as teams, serve on committees, are members of the same clubs, or are taking a class together can effectively use such distribution lists for sharing information and communications rapidly between members of the group.

- **Attaching files and documents to messages**: Even many frequent e-mail users are unaware of one of the most powerful capabilities of modern mailing programs—*file attachment*. Many e-mail programs in current use on campus computer systems allow the attaching of documents to electronic correspondence. With such programs, practically any file that can be stored on a computer may be sent along with your mail message to the recipient. These "attachment files" could be any document you have stored on your computer, such as a file generated by a word processor, a graphic created by desktop publishing software, or a computer program you wrote for a class.

When your e-mail message is sent, any files on your computer system which you've chosen to attach to it will ride along with the message through the Internet highways to its destination. When the individual(s) you have sent the mail to receive your message, they will also be delivered an electronic copy of any computer documents you attached to the correspondence. Attached files are usually delivered *exactly* as sent.

Examples of some file types which a student could attach to an e-mail message would include various word processing documents (such as reports, term papers, class notes, and schedules), electronic spreadsheets, graphics, pictures, diagrams, mailing lists, sounds, music, databases, charts, presentations, and computer programs, including software utilities and *shareware*.

2.3   How E-mail Works

Although this is not a book focused on the technology behind the workings of the Internet, it may be helpful to discuss the general process by which electronic mail is exchanged using this medium.

For example, when a student types a message into a typical mail program, and sends it through the Internet, a number of events are happening "behind the scenes." Let's say, for a moment, that John is a student at a college on the west coast of the United States and is sending an e-mail message to Mary, who attends school in a different region of the country. The following list of events is typical of the processes which normally occur during an exchange of electronic correspondence:

1. John starts his computer and logs on to his campus computer system. (He enters his user name and password to gain entry.)

2. Next, he types a command to enter the electronic mail system. This starts a program which allows John to send or receive mail through the local campus network and via the Internet.

3. John enters a command to the mail program to compose a *new message* for sending. A portion of his computer screen becomes available for him to type his message and edit it to his satisfaction. He also notifies the program who the intended recipient of the message is by entering Mary's e-mail address into the header portion of the message entry form on the screen.

4. John sends the message to Mary. (On most mailing programs, this requires only the press of a key or click of the mouse to accomplish.)

5. The message is converted by John's computer into electronic form. (Computers work with information in electronic form only. Luckily, they work with this electronic information at "blinding speed" and near-perfect reliability, which makes possible the Internet, e-mail, and all other forms of electronic communications.)

6. Since John's computer is programmed to be connected to the Internet, it automatically converts the e-mail message into a form suitable for transmission on the Internet called *TCP/IP*. (TCP/IP will not be explained here in any technical sense, but can be thought of as a special electronic language used for information communicated through the Internet.)

7. John's computer sends the message (now translated into electronic TCP/IP form) along its way toward its destination through the Internet.

Part of the message that John sent included a *header*, which included Mary's e-mail address. This information is used to route the message correctly toward its destination (Mary's computer).

8. Eventually, after a few minutes or hours, the message arrives at a special computer on the Internet known as a *mail server*. The mail server is where the computer system on Mary's campus receives and deposits electronic mail for its users. This mail server may be a special computer connected directly to Mary's campus network, or could very possibly be a different computer indirectly attached to it via the Internet.

Mail server computers can be visualized as performing the functions of "electronic post offices." They are dedicated to gathering up and storing electronic mail from the Internet for their users, as well as to sending out mail to destinations on the Internet. Every student with an Internet account and e-mail privileges has access (through the mail program) to a mail server computer which is used for sending, receiving, and storing electronic correspondence.

9. At some later time, Mary decides to check her *e-mailbox* for any new mail which may have arrived since she last checked. She logs on to the Internet and starts her mail program. (It doesn't matter that Mary's campus computer network is markedly different from the type John uses—e-mail can be shared between users of the Internet regardless of the type or brand of computer hardware or software they are using.)

10. Mary reviews a list displayed on her computer screen of all new mail messages which have arrived recently, and notices that John has mailed her. (Behind the scenes, mail was transported to Mary's computer from her mailbox on the mail server computer used by her campus network.)

11. Mary *opens* the mail message (displays it on her computer screen) and reads it. At this point, Mary can *print* the message if she wishes, *save* it on a computer disk for future reference, immediately *respond* to it, *forward* it to another person, or *delete* it.

Messages are routed through the Internet to the recipient's computer through a series of intermediate computers in the network. These server computers, operational 24 hours a day, have the responsibility of receiving, storing, and relaying electronic mail along the Internet highways to their destinations.

These computer servers pass the message from one to another in "bucket brigade" fashion, and ultimately deliver it to the intended recipient(s). Different types of servers perform a variety of important functions on the Internet (such as providing information to clients that request it or relaying messages to other computers). Mail server computers, as discussed earlier, perform the functions of an electronic post office.

E-mail communication works in an analogous fashion to the telephone which everyone is familiar with. When a person makes a telephone call, the voice (after being converted into electronic form) is sent through a series of intermediate relay stations until it reaches the receiver of the person at the other end of the connection, where it is converted back into an audible voice.

An advantage of e-mail over the use of the telephone to communicate is that the receiver of the message *does not have to be present* when the message is sent. Therefore, you can send e-mail through the Internet at a time which is convenient for you, and the recipients of your mail can pick up their messages at the times most convenient for them.

As discussed earlier, e-mail messages are stored for individuals in dedicated mail server computers, which are usually online 24 hours a day. Incoming mail is safely saved in these computers until it is picked up by the intended recipients. This feature of Internet e-mail allows you to keep regular correspondence with an individual, without worrying about setting up schedules for when you are both free to communicate at the same time.

2.4 Advantages of E-mail for Students

Gaining facility with e-mail can.be a significant benefit for students desiring to improve their chances for academic success. Listed here are a few examples of how this communication and information-sharing medium can be used in an educational setting.

- **E-mail to classmates:** You can easily share class notes, "handouts," and other supplementary materials with others. If you're working together with classmates on a project, it's easy to keep the members of the team updated on the progress of the assignment.

- **E-mail to students at other institutions:** You can share ideas for research or collaborate very efficiently in other ways with students at other schools by exchanging correspondence through e-mail. Members of national student organizations can also maintain contact with each other and exchange news and information using the Internet as a reliable communication medium.

- **E-mail to researchers in your field of interest:** Those pursuing research studies or who need information for a term paper or project should consider e-mailing a researcher or expert in their field of interest. An earnest request by a student for advice or assistance in academic matters may be directed to certain individuals through Internet e-mail. For example, when pursuing graduate studies at a particular institution, a prospective student may wish to ask faculty members teaching courses in their academic discipline for information about the graduate program offered at that institution.

- **E-mail to college admissions departments:** If you're preparing to enter college or a professional school, it is frequently possible to obtain admissions information directly through e-mail correspondence with admissions or guidance offices. Many academic institutions now have a World Wide Web "site" which may include e-mail addresses for contacts regarding admissions information.

  As you explore the Web (which we will do in our tours section later in this text), you will discover that some colleges have included Web-based "forms" where a prospective student may enter a request for admissions and related information. After clicking the Send button on the computer screen, the request will be routed directly to the school through the Internet, and the information will often be returned to the interested student via e-mail or by regular postal mail ("snail mail").

- **E-mail to your instructors:** If your instructors have e-mail accessibility (which many currently do), they may be willing to respond to your questions regarding material discussed in class through electronic correspondence. It is certainly important to consult with your instructor first, however, before assuming e-mail is appropriate for that purpose. Many instructors still prefer (and with good reason) to see a student one-on-one in their office when discussing academic matters. Nevertheless, an instructor may be more than willing to review via e-mail work in progress, such as a term paper you're writing, research you're gathering, a project underway, or just general questions about the class, assignment, or future exams.

  Many instructors are now using modern electronic communications tools in their approach to education, and distribute class notes, lecture materials, syllabi, review sheets, and even exams by Internet e-mail. Some colleges are using e-mail to deliver entire courses over the Internet! Lectures are distributed in text (and sometimes audio) forms, allowing students to receive course materials, lecture notes, and assignments and take exams through e-mail. A recent and growing approach to instructional delivery entitled *distance education* is based on similar techniques for the use of communications technology in learning.

- **E-mail to your future employers:** Investigating employment opportunities and applying for jobs using e-mail has become quite common. Many companies seeking employees now accept résumés through e-mail, as it can be an efficient way to gather credentials from prospective candidates for employment openings from a large pool of qualified applicants. If you're near graduation or are seeking career opportunities, the Internet may be a fruitful area for you to begin your search. Also, if you're looking for part-time employment while in school, or desire information on internships and practicums, submitting your credentials via e-mail is becoming an acceptable success strategy. Later in this text, we will introduce some areas on the World Wide Web which link directly to resources on the Internet valuable for students investigating employment opportunities.

- **E-mail to yourself:** There can be some distinct advantages to sending regular e-mail messages and notes to *yourself*. For example, it is easy to keep an online academic journal of your progress in college classes by making a habit of writing your thoughts, ideas, and notes into the computer and mailing them to yourself. Electronic mail messages are stamped by date and time, so it is possible to review your journal entries at a later time and compile a "progress report" based on these notes you've kept.

2.5 How to Get Your Own E-mail Address

In order to get your own address for receiving electronic mail over the Internet, you will need to have an account set up for you on the campus computer system. At some colleges and universities, accounts are available for all students, while other schools may require you to enroll in a computer class or pay a special fee for those privileges. Consult your computer class instructor, or visit the computing center on your campus for specific information regarding the requirements for Internet access by students.

An account will allow you privileges to access your school's computer system as well as the Internet. Usually, you will be assigned a user name for your account, which you will need to enter into the computer when logging on to the system. Your user name is often related to your real name in some way, such as an initial followed by your last name (*with no spaces in between*). For example, the student named Jack Paulson may be assigned the user name jpaulson, jpaulso, or jackp (note that sometimes the name may be abbreviated in some way).

Along with your user name, you will also usually need a *password* to gain entry into the system. The password ensures that only *you* will be able to access the computer files you create and store in the directories assigned to your account. Others should not be able to read your e-mail or otherwise gain entry to any documents that you have stored on the system (unless you give them "permission rights"). Sometimes a temporary password (such as "student" or "newuser") is assigned to you when your account is initially set up. *It is important to learn how to change your password as soon as possible after you have logged on to the system with your new account.* Ask a lab attendant, or consult a system manual for information on selecting and changing your password for accessing the campus computer system.

Use a password that is easy for you to remember, *but that virtually no one else could possibly guess.* For that reason, don't use your girlfriend's or boyfriend's name (or the name of your cat or goldfish) for a password, because it is possible for illegal users—"crackers"—to easily gain entry into computer accounts with such obvious names for passwords. Use a mixture of uppercase and lowercase letters and special characters (such as a hyphen), and include at least one or two digits in the password if possible. *Remember not to forget your password.* Write your password down in a secure place—not in your class notebook, computer manuals, or textbook.

When you are provided with an account on your school's system, you will likely be assigned an e-mail address at that time. Frequently, your address will be in the form of

username@nameofcomputer.nameofschool.edu

For example, "Jack Paulson," who is using the computer network in the Physics Department at "Sunshine University," may be assigned an e-mail address similar to one of these following possibilities:

jackp@physics.sunshine.edu

jpaulson@physics.sunsh.edu

jpaulson@phys.sunshine.edu

jackp@physics.sshine.edu

jack_paulson@phys.sunshine.edu

Sometimes the name of the computer network is omitted, resulting in simpler e-mail addresses, such as:

jackp@sunshine.edu

jpaulson@sunsh.edu

jpaulson@sunshine.edu

(Note that in all cases the e-mail address ends with the .edu *suffix, which is a standard abbreviation for "educational institution.")*

2.6   How to Locate Someone Else's E-mail Address

If you would like to send e-mail to someone, you obviously need to know that person's e-mail address, just as you can't send a letter through the post office without an address placed on the envelope.

Here are some ways to locate others' e-mail addresses:

- Ask them! Although this may seem obvious, sometimes the best, and quickest, way to locate a person's e-mail address is to simply ask. By placing a phone call to an individual, or inquiring in person, you may find out this information directly. Keep a list of important e-mail addresses in a notebook, or store them in a computer file for easy access. Some e-mail programs allow you to keep an online address book designed for that purpose. Check the user's manual or online *Help* system.

- Check the campus e-mail directory. At many schools, the e-mail addresses of the students, faculty, and staff are listed in such directories, and they may be available both in printed form and online in the computer system. Schools which have established a World Wide Web or gopher site on the Internet frequently include e-mail addresses of faculty, staff, and students. In a later chapter of this text, we will discuss how to access the *Campus Wide Information System* (CWIS) which many schools have placed on the Internet, and which freely provide valuable information (such as e-mail addresses) to interested parties.

  The list of campus e-mail addresses may be available on the school's World Wide Web pages if the school has constructed and installed a Web site on the Internet. When visiting a school's Web page, you can often gain near-instant access to a wealth of information and news regarding that campus, including an online e-mail directory of students in attendance as well as the faculty and staff.

- Use the Internet. Many facilities and tools exist on the Internet which are designed to assist individuals in locating e-mail addresses. These "search engines" will attempt to locate an e-mail address by consulting very large directories which are maintained just for this purpose. Access to these address-searching facilities can be gained at various Web and gopher sites, and their use will be discussed in Chapters 4 and 6 of this text. Typically, an e-mail search engine will ask the user to enter as much information about the individual being sought as can be provided, such as first and last name, as well as the institution where attending or employed. The *Netfind* searching engine (which is accessible through the Web and gopher) is an example of a frequently used tool for locating e-mail addresses via the Internet.

2.7   Sending an E-mail Message

Fortunately, with most electronic mailing programs in current use, the process of sending an e-mail message is quite simple. The steps for sending e-mail over the Internet generally follow the procedure listed here:

1. The sender of the e-mail message logs on to a computer system and starts the mailing program.

   Due to the variety of different types of computers currently in use by students (from large mainframe systems to palmtop PCs) and the fact that many mailing programs are in existence, with new versions frequently being developed, this text cannot focus on any one type or brand of computer hardware or software. The discussion will be geared toward the general steps of using Internet e-mail, without getting bogged down by the details of particular systems in use.

2. In order to access the program to compose a new message for sending, the message sender clicks on New Message (or enters a similar command at the keyboard). As stated, since each mail program operates somewhat differently, specific commands cannot be outlined for each operation discussed.

3. The header portion of the message is filled in, starting with:

   • **To:** The user enters the *e-mail address* of the recipient in the To: line of the message header. (Obviously, you need to know the e-mail address of the person who will receive your mail message.)

A Word on E-mail Addresses

E-mail addresses at educational institutions follow the format:

username@ machine.domain.edu

where:

username is the log-in name of the Internet user,

machine is the name of the computer being used,

domain is the name of the institution, company, or facility which is "hosting" the user's account, and

.edu is an abbreviation for "educational institution."

An example of a mythical e-mail address for a user in the engineering department at the University of Michigan may be:

rjones@ engin.umich.edu

where *rjones* is the user's log-in name, *engin* corresponds to a computer server used by the engineering department, followed by *umich,* which is the domain name for the University of Michigan.

Commercial e-mail addresses end with the suffix *.com,* (rather than *.edu*), government institutions with *.gov* (see Figure 2.1), and military installations with *.mil.*

- **From:** This line states the mailing address of the *sender* of the message (which in most cases will be *you,* assuming you logged on to the system using your own account which includes personal e-mail privileges). Your e-mail address may be automatically filled in for you by many mailing programs. If you are using a nonpersonal account, you must enter it yourself. This portion of the message header is analogous to the "return address" placed on the envelope of a postal letter.

- **Subject:** In this line of the header, it is recommended that you enter a brief word or phrase corresponding to the subject of your message. The subject line gives the receiver of the message an idea of what is inside the electronic envelope that has been received from you by e-mail. (*Subject lines are usually short and to the point.*) Mailing programs allow users to quickly review and sort their e-mail messages by subject, date, or name of the sender.

- **Message body:** After the header information is entered, the user can type the message into the *editor* of the mail program. Simple mail program editors allow you only to enter and correct text, whereas others have many additional features such as cut and paste, spell-checking, and other capabilities designed to help the user in the mailing process. When the sender has entered the message (both the header and text body portion) and is satisfied the information entered is correct, the next step is to send the message.

4. When the message has been completed and has been checked for errors, the user can click the Send button (or press an appropriate Send key), and the electronic message will be routed into the Internet, where (hopefully) it will arrive in due course at its correct destination(s).

2.8   Reading Your Mail

As discussed earlier, electronic mail messages delivered through the Internet are stored in mail server computers until they are picked up by their intended recipients. When you start your mailing program, and are safely connected to the Internet, you may be notified by the program if you have any new mail that is waiting for you at your mail server. Sometimes the program will automatically retrieve from the server any new mail you've received and transfer it to a special file on your local computer system. In many programs, new mail is deposited into a special folder or mailbox on your computer with a corresponding title such as "New Mail," "In-Box," or "Unread Mail." Check the Help system on your mail program for specific information on the various commands used in its operation.

After logging on to the Internet and starting your mail program, new messages you've received since your last log-on will usually be shown in a list sorted by date and time of arrival. The subject lines of the message headers of all new mail you've received since you last checked your mail will be presented. At this point, you simply choose the message you wish to read and "open" it by clicking your mouse on it, selecting it through the keyboard and pressing Enter, entering its "message number," or by a similar command, depending on the mail program in use.

Not All Mail Programs Are Alike

As previously stated, different computer systems and e-mail software do not all function in the same way. Computer programs which display on-screen windows and use a mouse operate differently (and often more conveniently) than older systems which use text commands entered by the user at the keyboard. Modern e-mail software includes a number of features that older systems lacked, such as automatic saving of all sent messages, the capability of storing mail in folders, importing message text from other computer programs or files, sorting message lists, spell-checking, and integration with other Internet software tools such as Web browsers and newsgroup reading programs. *For specific information on the capabilities and usage of your mailing program, remember that most include a Help system designed to assist you in learning the program.*

After you've opened an e-mail message (displayed its contents on your computer screen) and read it, you will typically have a number of options as to what to do next, including the following:

- You can *transfer* that message from your in-box to a folder in your computer mailing system. Keeping your mail in folders allows you to organize your messages by subject, author, or date, allowing you to quickly access them at a later time. Although most mailing systems will keep mail you've read in your in-box for a certain length of time, it is a good practice to move important messages to a folder for safekeeping or otherwise save them for future reference. On your campus system, e-mail messages may be saved for several weeks (or until you manually delete them from your mailbox), but you may wish to check details on e-mail storage with your computer center personnel.

- If your mailing program allows copy and paste operations, such as those available on most modern computers, including Windows-based PCs, the Macintosh, and modern X-Windows-based Unix systems, it is very easy to *save* the contents of a message into a separate file. If you share the use of a computer with another student, or pick up your e-mail in the computer lab, it may be helpful to store a file of important mail messages on a removable "diskette" which you can keep with you or otherwise maintain in a safe place. Most modern computer systems have generic and easy-to-use text-editing programs which allow you to create and save text files that can be

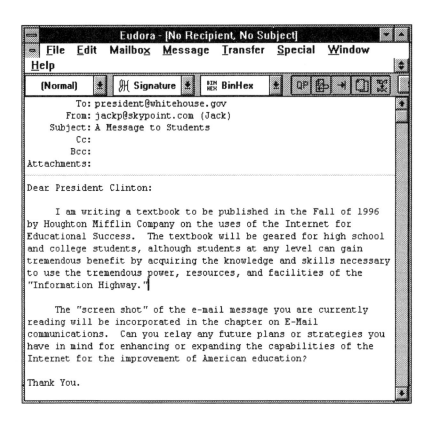

Fig. 2.1 Screen shot of an actual e-mail message sent to the White House

shared using standard copy and paste operations in your mailing program. *Consult your computer user's manual or Help menu for assistance.*

- You can *print* a "hard copy" of the message to read or refer to at a later time. (*It is worthwhile to print a copy of critical e-mail messages, or save them on a personal diskette which is stored in a safe place.*)

- You can *forward* the message to another person through the Internet. Most modern e-mail programs have a forwarding feature which allows a message to be quickly "re-sent" to another individual. After reading a new message, or reviewing a document stored in one of your mail folders, you often may be able to forward it by typing a key corresponding to the Forward command (or clicking the Forward button), entering the e-mail address of the new recipient, and selecting the Send command or button.

You should be very cautious in the use of this feature! If you receive mail of a personal or private nature, it is unethical to forward it to another indi-

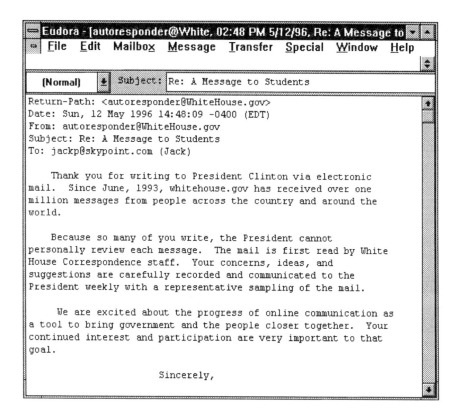

Fig. 2.2 Actual response to the previous e-mail message to the White House

vidual unless you have received permission from the person who originated that message. *E-mail should be assumed private unless stated otherwise by the sender.* However, if an individual mails you information you
may find valuable to share with someone else, don't hesitate to ask the
sender of that message for permission to forward it. One of the great advantages of Internet-based communications is the ease by which information can be relayed to interested individuals, allowing resources to be
shared among many people in a very efficient and cost-effective manner.

- You can *reply* to the message. If, after reading an e-mail message, you
  wish to issue the sender a return response, a Reply command is available
  in most e-mail programs for this purpose. While your mail program editor
  is displaying a message, select the Reply button (or press the appropriate
  keystroke), enter the subject of your responding message into the header,
  type your message, and select the Send command to route it back through

the Internet to its destination. Direct replies to e-mail messages frequently include Re: in the subject line of the header (see Figure 2.2).

Selecting the Reply option on many modern e-mail programs will automatically include the sender's original message in the body of your return response; usually each line is preceded by a special character such as >. *This feature is included as a convenience for you, as it can facilitate quicker replies by not forcing you to retype those parts of the sender's message which you are referencing in your response.* (With most e-mail programs which include this capability, this feature can be turned off if the user so desires.) Selecting the Options (or similar) menu item or button will allow you to customize the functions of your mail program to suit your own preferences and requirements.

- You can *delete* the message permanently from your mailbox. As mentioned previously, e-mail messages are automatically stored for a certain length of time on many e-mail systems. As a student user of the Internet, you will notice that messages will tend to accumulate in your in-box over time (if you don't transfer them to other folders or remove them). The solution to an overflowing mailbox or folder is the Delete (or related) command, which does as you would expect: it permanently removes a message from your e-mailbox.

Since e-mail messages consume valuable disk space on a computer system, most students are allocated a limited amount of storage for their saved mail. Important mail should be saved on a separate disk or printed, and other messages should be regularly removed from your mailbox using the Delete command in your mailing program.

If you aren't sure which command to use to perform a particular mailing function, always remember to check the documentation for the program and system you are using. Documentation (including the user's manual), whether it is in printed or online form, allows you to look up information on the sequence of commands, keystrokes, or "mouse clicks" to use to perform the various program functions. (*As stated earlier, mail programs differ widely in their operation, although the basic functions performed remain quite similar. It's not practical to outline in this text the exact methods the many mailing programs use to perform the various operations.*)

2.9 Sending Mail to Multiple Recipients

If you are interested in sending a copy of an e-mail message to a second person simultaneously with the original, there is an easy way to do it. In the header part of your mail message there is an additional line or two for sending carbon copies. A "carbon copy" is an identical copy of an e-mail message which is routed to a second individual.

To send a carbon copy of a message, simply type in the e-mail address of the individual who is to receive the second copy in the Cc: line of the message header. After your message is sent, *two* copies will be routed to destinations over the Internet: one to the original recipient, and a copy to the individual you named on the Cc: line of the header.

With some e-mail programs, there is a second carbon copy line in the message header. The Bcc: line refers to the address to send a "blind carbon copy," which is a message copy sent to a second individual, *without the awareness of the primary message recipient.* Sending blind carbon copies is considered by many in the Internet community to be unethical, as the original recipient of the message is *completely unaware* that a copy of the message received has also been routed to another individual.

It is also possible to send mail to *several* addresses at one time, in a single "group mailing" of an e-mail message. Check your mail program documentation for setting up a distribution list, which is a facility included with many modern e-mail programs designed for this purpose. By entering the e-mail addresses of each individual in the group onto a list, it is possible to distribute mail automatically to all of them at once! Also, by giving that distribution list a *distribution list name*, the entire list of the members' e-mail addresses can be stored on the computer system and recalled at a later time. In the future, mail messages can be sent to all the individuals in the group by a single mailing to the distribution list.

For example, an instructor with several classes could put the e-mail addresses of the members of each class onto separate distribution lists. If that instructor desires to send frequent e-mail messages (such as lecture notes or assignments) to all members of a class at once, it is only necessary to recall the name of the class's distribution list and send a single mail message to all students in that class at once. If new individuals are admitted to a particular class, or other members leave, the instructor only needs to update the distribution list when changes occur.

As a second example, suppose you are the head of a campus committee and you wish to send meeting notices to all members of the committee on a regular basis using e-mail. By entering the e-mail addresses of all the members of the committee onto a distribution list, you can very efficiently send notices to all members of the committee in a single mailing.

If your e-mail program supports them, using distribution lists can certainly save you time when sending identical messages to several members of a group. You will be spared the chore of repetitively entering the addresses of all individuals in the group when you wish to distribute a copy of a message to each of its members. *Also, as new members join or old members leave the group, it's only necessary to update your distribution list to keep your mailing addresses current.*

2.10   Attaching Documents to Messages

One of the most powerful features of modern e-mail software is the capability of attaching electronic documents of virtually any type to an e-mail message. File attachment is a simple process of selecting the files in your computer system which you would like to send to the recipient along with your message. In the mail programs which support this feature, there is typically a menu option or command such as Attach File, where the names of the files you select for attachment will be listed in the header portion of your e-mail message. After sending your message, the attached file(s) will be routed (along with your message, of course) to the recipient(s). This powerful capability of current e-mail software allows a student to use e-mail not only for communication, but also for exchanging and sharing files and documents of any type that can be stored on a computer (see Figure 2.3).

As the following examples illustrate, e-mail users who have access to mailing software with attachment capability can easily distribute and share the following types of files and documents with their e-mail messages:

- **Word processing documents**, including term papers, projects, reports, class notes, application and cover letters, résumés, and other documents created on a word processor, can be attached to e-mail. Attachment capability allows the student to easily collaborate with other students on a project or submit their materials for review or comment by others. Instructors with Internet access, and who regularly use e-mail communications, may be amenable to the acceptance of class assignments, projects, and papers attached to e-mail messages by students. In many cases, it is helpful if the recipient of the document has access to the same word processor used to create it, although modern software applications—including word processors—typically allow the "importing" of documents stored in a range of different document formats.

- **Spreadsheets and databases** may be included with e-mail as attachments. Assignments, project results, and research data collected or analyzed can be easily sent to a faculty member, project leader, supervisor, research collaborator, or any other Internet user for review. Business, financial, and scientific data are often collected and analyzed in spreadsheet format.

- **Graphics files,** including charts, diagrams, digital photographs, clip art, maps, and many other applications of computer graphics, can be readily attached to e-mail messages. A large variety of graphics files is freely available on the Internet for users to download to their computers. A student artist, for example, could create a piece of artwork, scan it into a computer file, and share it with an interested person across the world using Internet e-mail.

- **Sound and music files** can be easily shared between listeners by attachment to e-mail. As the sound card has become a very commonly included accessory in many personal computer systems, more students are sharing musical creations with each other by distributing electronic files through the Internet. For example, musical instrument digital interface (MIDI) files consist of musical information stored in an efficient electronic form, which can be easily sent as an e-mail attachment. Also, multimedia "presentation" files, which frequently include the sounds of music and voice narration (integrated with visually appealing graphics), can be distributed among users through files attached to accompanying e-mail messages.

Computer programs can also be transferred between Internet users as attachments. Please keep in mind that it is illegal to copy many types of commercial software, and the penalties can be quite strict for engaging in that activity. At the very least, you may lose your Internet account and e-mail privileges for copying many types of "protected" software. Programs you write yourself for class assignments, projects, or work may certainly be attached to e-mail for review or testing by others.

BEWARE OF VIRUSES

It can be dangerous to open a document or start a computer program which has been received through the Internet from any unknown source. For example, in April 1997, a program with the title "AOL 4FREE" was being sent to thousands of Internet users via attachment to unsolicited e-mail messages (that is, junk mail). When this document was opened by unwary recipients, it caused the entire contents of their disk drives to be destroyed—causing irreparable damage to the files stored on their computer systems! Such "virus-infected" programs exist in widespread numbers on the Internet—and can be easily spread among computers using e-mail attachment and FTP (see Section 6.3).

Adhering to the following suggestions will increase your protection against damage inflicted by software viruses:

- Always keep a current backup of important files stored off of your computer on diskettes.

- Remain wary of any documents or files received from individuals (especially of an unknown identity or origin) on the Internet!

- Ensure that the latest virus protection software is installed on any computer system you use which connects to the Internet. Consult with your computer system administrator, lab attendant, or instructor for information on this issue.

- If your mail reading program allows the receiving of attached files, be certain that it will not *automatically* run programs or open attached documents. Mail readers which include this capability should have an option to turn this feature off. Consult the program documentation or computer system personnel if you need assistance. *The same holds for other Internet client applications, including Web browsers, gopher programs, FTP clients, and the like.*

- Keep abreast of the latest news regarding computer viruses. If you have access to newsgroups (see Chapter 5), check the comp.virus group occasionally for information and discussion regarding this issue.

2.11   Organizing Your Mail with Folders

If you receive a large amount of e-mail, and unless you delete messages after you have read them, your e-mailbox may gradually fill up with a large quantity of mail. Many e-mailing programs allow you to organize your mail into manageable electronic folders for ease of access to your saved messages at a later time. E-mail folders are analogous to the cardboard file folders used to separate paper documents in a typical office filing cabinet.

If you correspond regularly with more than one person, you may wish to set up a mail folder for each of these individuals (assuming that your mailing software supports this feature). This will assist you in organizing your mail and referencing it at a later time. Check your e-mail program documentation for this valuable feature. Keep in mind, however, that many students are allocated only a certain maximum amount of computer disk storage space for saving old mail, so you may wish to keep only those messages you will need to reference at a later time. Also, as discussed previously, very important e-mail messages should be printed or copied to a separate file or diskette and saved in a secure place.

2.12   Subscribing to Discussion Lists

A discussion list is a group of individuals who use the Internet to share e-mail regarding a subject of mutual interest. Individuals who have subscribed to a discussion list related to a given topic are able to read mail contributed by other members of the group regarding that topic. When a message is *posted* to the list by any one member, all members of the group will receive a copy of that message in their e-mailboxes. Every member of the discussion list has the capabilities of both sending messages to and receiving mail from the group's other participants. Individuals can very efficiently share information with each other about mutual areas of study, research, or personal interest using discussion lists on the Internet.

In order for you to become a participant in a discussion list, it is necessary to subscribe to the list by e-mail. A subscription is simply an e-mail message that you send to an address of a special computer on the Internet which will manage all the mail shared by members of the list. Usually, the computer distributing the e-mail between members of a discussion list is running a dedicated program for that purpose called a *listserv*. You needn't understand how listserv programs operate to join and participate in a discussion list over the Internet, but a brief analogy may help explain the process.

Suppose you wanted to exchange lecture notes taken by a group of students in a college class who have formed a study group. If all members of this group were to copy their class notes on a daily basis and e-mail them to the other students in the group, everyone would have access to each other's notes—which could be mutually beneficial when studying the subject matter. However, all students in the group would need to keep a *current* copy of the names and addresses of *all* of the other members. Also, each student in the group would be responsible for sending notes to every other student on the list on a daily basis!

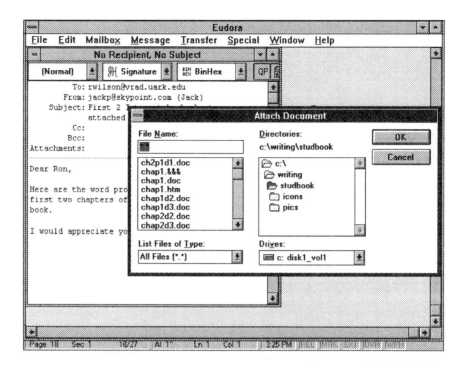

Fig. 2.3 Adding an attachment document to an e-mail message

Management of the names and addresses of the list members could pose yet a more serious problem. If new students joined the group—or others dropped out—the mailing list would need to be maintained by *every* student in the group. For a small list of members this may not be an issue of significance, but for very large groups (such as the many thousands of members typically sharing mail through Internet-based discussion lists) it would be a tremendously difficult situation to manage—especially since such lists usually allow individuals to join or withdraw their membership from the group at any time.

An efficient solution to these problems is to designate one individual to be the "list manager and message distributor" for all members of the group. For example, in a study group, if one student had the *sole* responsibility of maintaining the mailing list and sending out all copies of notes to group members, individual students would be responsible only for making one copy of their notes and sending it to the distributor on a daily basis. This is the basis for the operation of *listserv* discussion lists on the Internet. The listserv computer acts as the distributor of all messages shared between group members. Sending a message to *all* members of the group is a simple matter of sending *one* message to the listserv computer, which is then responsible for copying and distributing that mailing to all the other members on the list.

The steps to participating in Internet discussion lists are as follows:

1. Browse a comprehensive index of mailing lists for one that matches an interest area of yours. Please be aware that there are literally *tens of thousands* of available lists on the Internet to choose from! An index of discussion lists can be acquired from various sources, including books, as well as on the Internet itself. Your computer center may have a printed copy of such a list, so you may wish to check for one at your campus computer center, or ask a computer lab assistant if one is available.

    An alternative source for an index of discussion lists is to browse the World Wide Web, where many such "lists of lists" are maintained at various Web sites. For example, entering

    ### listserv index biology

    into a *search engine* form on the Web may possibly lead you directly to a page with an index of sites which can link you to information regarding biology discussion lists on the Internet (including subscription information). The Web search engines and their uses are described in detail in Chapter 4.

2. After finding a discussion list which you wish to join, make a note of *two e-mail addresses* which will correspond to most discussion lists that are maintained by listserv computer servers:

    The first address is a *listserv* mailing address, which is where you will send your e-mail message to subscribe to the list. Later, if you decide to withdraw your name from the list, you will send your "unsubscribing" message to this same address.

    The second list address is the one you will use *after* you have been notified that your subscription to the list has been received and approved. This address will be where you will send any e-mail messages you wish to share with members of the group. Many new listserv users (often called "newbies") make the mistake of sending messages to the wrong address. For example, after joining the list, they often send messages for posting to the list to the first e-mail address described (which is used for subscribing or unsubscribing to the list—not sending mail to the list members).

3. After subscribing to a list, the listserv computer will usually send you a *verification message* via e-mail, informing you that your subscription has been approved and that you are now a member of that list. If your subscription is not accepted (*usually because your subscription message was not correctly written*), the listserv will notify you of the problem.

4. It may take from a few minutes to several hours before a listserv computer on the Internet processes your subscription and verifies your membership in a discussion list. Once approved, you will begin to receive e-mail from the listserv from other members of the group. Remember that the messages posted to a discussion list are meant for all interested members of the group, and are not to be focused toward any particular individual. *Personal comments or notes which are to be shared with only one or two individuals should be sent using a standard e-mail message, not through a discussion group mailing list.*

    Depending on how active the list is, you may receive many such postings shared by the group's members on a daily basis, and your e-mailbox may quickly be filled with messages from the discussion list. Some colleges discourage (or outright prohibit) the joining of discussion lists by students for this reason. (This can be unfortunate, because participating in academically related discussion groups on the Internet can enhance the educational environment for many students, allowing them to share in conversations in many important areas relevant to their learning needs—both academic and personal.)

5. Before sending your own messages to the list members, it is advisable to read the postings submitted by others for a few days to get a feel for the nature of the conversations in process and some of the topics currently under discussion. Also, you may inadvertently join a discussion group which is not appropriate to your interests, and you will soon become aware of this as you read the messages shared between the group's members.

6. If, after reading e-mail messages being shared by members of a list, you would like to contribute your own comments, feedback, or information regarding a subject relevant to the group, it's a simple matter to post a message to the list. Start your e-mail program, and enter the "list address" (*the second e-mail address described*) in the To: line of your e-mail message header. Write your message, click the Send button (or press the appropriate key), and your comments will be routed to the other list members through the listserv computer via the Internet.

There is a tremendous range of topics carried by the many thousands of currently active discussion lists on the Internet. Regardless of your specific areas of interest (academic or personal), there is very likely a list suitable for you to join. As previously mentioned, it is advantageous to consult an index of available discussion lists to gain a perspective on the voluminous range of discussion topics covered in these groups through the facilities of the Internet.

Consulting a Discussion Group Index

In the example shown in Figure 2.4, I used a World Wide Web browser to consult an index of available discussion lists on the Internet. After reviewing this list of lists, I located the following Web page with subscription information for a list on classical music.

It is very convenient that large indexes of the many thousands of currently active discussion lists are maintained on the Internet. A Web browser is an exceptionally valuable tool for locating information about lists related to topics of interest. Finding information on the Web is discussed in the next chapter of this text.

You can see that in order to join the discussion list on classical music, it is necessary only to send a single e-mail message to the appropriate listserv address in the following form:

Message Header:

To: listserv@brownvm.brown.edu   **From: My e-mail address** (*usually filled in automatically by the mail program*)   **Subject:** (*leave this line blank . . .*)

Message Body Text:

sub CLASSM-L Joe Smith

Note that the command **sub** in the message body is an abbreviation for "subscribe to list . . ." Following the **sub** is the name of the list, which in this case is the classical music list: CLASSM-L. Finally, you need to enter only your first and last name. (Note that the subject line is blank and ignored by the listserv.)

After I send this e-mail message, my subscription will be processed by a listserv computer, and I should soon become a member of this list, whose members discuss topics related to classical music. If, at any time in the future, I decide to withdraw my membership from this list, I only need to send a single unsubscribe message to the same listserv address I used when joining it. Following the exact procedure as before, but replacing the **sub** line in the message text with the single word **unsub** (*unsubscribe*), and sending the message, I should soon be notified that I am no longer a member of the classical music list.

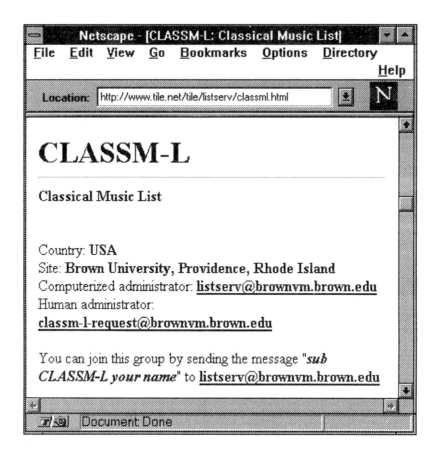

Fig. 2.4 Subscription information for a classical music discussion list

Posting a message to the members of the discussion list is as easy as sending an e-mail message to the list address for messages to be shared with the group (the *second* e-mail address discussed previously).

Referring to the previous example, I could send a message to the classical music list in the following way:

To: classm-l@brownvm.brown.edu *(Note the use of the "list address")*

From: My e-mail address *(usually filled in automatically by the mail program)*

Subject: Beethoven's "Moonlight Sonata"

Would anyone know of a recent digital recording on CD of Beethoven's "Moonlight Sonata" for classical guitar? Thank you.

A Personal Bias by the Author

Two days after posting the subscription to the classical music discussion list, I had already received 197 e-mail messages from members of the group, completely flooding my e-mailbox! Many of the postings received did not relate to my specific interests in classical music, and I needed to take several minutes of time to read and subsequently delete a large number of these messages from my mailbox. Although discussion lists have their value, *it is my opinion that Usenet newsgroups (discussed in Chapter 5) are a preferable means for exchanging information between groups of Internet users.*

While browsing the messages posted to newsgroups, the user has the option to ignore messages of no particular interest. Space is not wasted on the local computer system for the large majority of messages which may not be relevant to the reader, and time is also saved in the process.

Listserv-based discussion lists can often result in a "flooding" of the mailbox by a large number of postings which may not be of interest to a discussion group's member. Also, students are allotted only a maximum amount of storage for e-mail, and a very active discussion group can easily result in excessive use of a student's e-mail resources.

2.13   Other Forms of Internet Communication

E-mail is certainly not the only means of communicating with other individuals over the Internet, although it is (by a huge margin) the most common. In fact, the Internet information highways are used primarily for exchanging text-based e-mail messages, in spite of the many other powerful tools available on it, including FTP, telnet, gopher, Usenet (newsgroups), and the World Wide Web.

As discussed previously, an excellent form of communication between groups of individuals mutually interested in a particular topic is through the Usenet newsgroups via the Internet. Newsgroups are giant electronic bulletin boards which are browsed by sometimes many thousands of individuals worldwide on a frequent basis. Messages can be posted on newsgroup bulletin boards by any interested students who have newsgroup access privileges along with their Internet accounts. Newsgroups perform a function similar to the listserv mailing lists discussed previously, although e-mail is generally not used for posting and reading messages to Usenet. A special "client program" is usually used by the user to contribute to, and access information from, the newsgroup bulletin boards. Communicating through the newsgroups will be discussed in detail in Chapter 5.

Chat groups are another form of communication growing in popularity. Internet users connect with each other, establish the line of communication, and are able to carry on a conversation by typing messages to each other in real time, which means the conversation takes place as it happens, sometimes with a short delay as the information is routed through the Internet to its destination. Chat groups enable students to converse with other individuals worldwide. For example, an American student desiring to improve ability in conversational Spanish could establish contact with an individual in Spain using a "chatting program" over the Internet, carry on the conversation in the foreign tongue, and improve Spanish-speaking abilities significantly.

IRC (Internet Relay Chat) is the most popular form of online chat system in current use by students. Currently, this medium is used primarily for social purposes, but there are many possible applications of IRC for education. The IRC is rarely used for research or academic purposes at the present time (although it certainly could be), so this text will not discuss this Internet facility in detail.

Students interested in IRC can easily find information on this topic from the Web using a browser. Typing **FAQ IRC** (FAQ is an abbreviation for "frequently asked questions") into one of the search engines of the Web should return a list of many Web sites to explore relating to this online chat facility. The Web search engines, including the presentation of examples of their use, will be discussed in detail in Chapter 4.

Very recently, multimedia-based chat systems have become popular. With a sound card installed on a computer, and by adding special software, audio can be exchanged in real time over the Internet, allowing users to communicate worldwide in a CB radio fashion. Though it is currently more in an experimental stage, future applications of this technology in education make it a worthy subject for interested students to investigate.

Although it can be a waste of valuable resources, it is even possible to send *video* across the Internet (in real time). Many student Internet users are actively experimenting with this newer technology. By attaching a video camera to a special piece of hardware installed on the computer, users can exchange video with other Internet users across the world. The applications of "video teleconferencing" for education are formidable, but the demands placed by this technology on limited Internet resources is most significant, especially because millions more Internet users are logging on each year!

2.14 E-mail Security

It is important to keep in mind that electronic mail is *not* a secure means for exchanging communications between individuals. Unlike postal letters, where strict laws exist prohibiting the unauthorized reading of someone else's mail, it is very possible that your e-mail could be seen and read by other individuals without your consent! Since Internet-based e-mail messages often pass through several computer servers before reaching their destination, it is possible for unscrupulous individuals to gain access to information stored in these systems, including your private e-mail messages. Highly personal or sensitive information should *not* be sent through Internet e-mail at the present time, although methods have been developed to encrypt messages for adding security. Privacy can be easily invaded, however, so be very careful of the content of the e-mail you exchange with others, and *never* assume that only the intended recipient of your messages will have access to them!

2.15 Notes on Using Program Documentation

At different points in this text, a reference is made to the *documentation* of the various computer programs discussed for use in accessing and retrieving information from the Internet. "Program documentation" typically refers to the documents which describe how to use the software, including the user's manual. In most Internet applications software developed in recent years, an online Help facility is usually included with the program. *It is important to remember to consult the documentation for any software you will be using in your explorations on the Internet.*

Accessing online assistance through the Help facility is usually a simple matter of pressing a special key (such as F1, or Alt+h) or of selecting the appropriate

Help option from the program's menu selection bar. This facility enables you to easily locate specific details describing the commands used in operating the program, as well as general reference information which may be a valuable resource if you have questions or problems while using the software.

Modern Help systems typically arrange the information by subject, and many include a comprehensive index and sometimes a "search" facility for looking up information related to a specific topic or command. In most cases, there is *no better way* to gain familiarity with the commands used in operating a program than by spending some time reviewing the information presented in the Help system, as well as any printed documentation that is available.

It is important, and can be quite productive, to spend a significant amount of time exploring the documentation included with any computer software you plan to use on a regular basis. *Remember that these resources were developed solely for the purpose of assisting you in the use of the program.*

Regarding the printed manual, it is unfortunate but true that often it may not be available *when you need it most.* If you are accessing the Internet in a computer lab at school, it may be possible to ask a lab assistant for help in the use of Internet applications programs, or you may need to ask for help in locating any available user's manuals (if they exist). Otherwise, don't forget to look for a Help facility, or online reference manual, when you are actually using the program—to guide you with questions or problems which may arise.

Summary

E-mail is a powerful, fast, and reliable form of text-based communications which can be of significant value to students. Sending e-mail is simple: enter the address of the recipient, a subject line, and the text of your message, and select the Send command. Mail is delivered to mail server computers on the Internet, which serve as electronic post offices for their users.

There is a significant number of useful applications of e-mail for students, including the sharing of class notes, research information, and data; collaborating on projects, teams, and committees; and sending and receiving correspondence with other students off-campus, or with professionals in the student's field.

It's easy to send multiple copies of e-mail using the Cc: (carbon copy) line of the message header. Also, distribution lists can be set up with most modern programs for performing mass mailings. Documents can be attached to e-mail messages for convenient file transfer among Internet users. Folders make organizing e-mail messages more manageable. Discussion lists allow a number of Internet users to share mail regarding a specific topic or area of interest to the list subscribers. Chat programs are a means for communicating in real time with another Internet user. Internet Relay Chat (IRC) is a popular means of communicating between students over the Internet, although it is used primarily for social, rather than academic, purposes at the present time.

Review Questions

1. Where is mail stored on the Internet before the recipient opens and reads it?

2. What is the purpose of the subject line of the mail message header?

3. List five advantages of e-mail communication over the use of the telephone to exchange information with another student.

4. Explain why e-mail messages are "well audited."

5. What information is often automatically added to a *reply* message in many modern e-mail programs?

6. Why should messages be *deleted* from your in-box on a regular basis?

7. List some uses not listed in the text for the sending of e-mail to *yourself.*

8. Explain how you would use a distribution list to work on a joint project with several members of your class.

9. What is the main purpose for the inclusion of Help systems on computer software applications (such as mail programs)?

10. What is it necessary for you to have before you can be assigned your own e-mail address?

11. Discuss methods for finding someone's e-mail address.

12. What is the purpose of the Bcc: line of an e-mail message header?

13. List some examples where attaching documents to your e-mail could be used in a school setting.

14. What are the purposes of the two e-mail addresses often needed to join and participate in discussion lists over the Internet?

15. What information is in the body of an e-mail message sent for subscribing to a listserv discussion list?

16. What command is sent to a listserv to cancel your subscription to a discussion list?

17. State two disadvantages of using listserv discussion lists for communicating information with groups of Internet users.

18. List two examples of multimedia-based communications over the Internet.

19. Name one disadvantage of exchanging video communications with other Internet users.

20. Explain why one should be careful in sending private messages over Internet e-mail.

Exercises

1. Send an e-mail message to yourself, outlining the key points discussed in this chapter. After sending it, print it and keep a copy for yourself.

2. Outline five ways that you could personally use e-mail in your academic studies or research.

3. After consulting a list of lists, subscribe to a discussion list of your choosing. If your mail program supports it, set up a mail folder for that list, and transfer into it all mail received from that discussion group.

4. Write a schedule of your next week's activities into a word processing program. If your mail program supports it, send the document as an attached file to a friend or classmate with e-mail access. Ask your friend to send a schedule back to you in the same way.

5. Form a study group with at least two friends with e-mail accounts for discussing your Internet experiences as you read each chapter of this text.

Chapter 3

How the Internet Works

3.1   Overview

In this chapter, we will present an overview of the structure of the Internet information highways. An analogy is presented, comparing the Internet with the highways and roads that have been designed for vehicular traffic. Resource types on the Internet are discussed, as are the software tools needed to access them. "Client–server" technology is presented to describe the design of Internet software tools. Most tools for accessing Internet resources come in pairs, consisting of a client and a server program. Internet site names and addresses are explained, and access to sites through the Web using URLs completes the discussion.

3.2   What Is a Computer Network?

A network is simply an arrangement of a number of computers so that they can share information (communicate) with each other in an efficient way. Communication "pathways" are made between the various computers in the network so that the information being shared can flow smoothly between the senders and receivers of that information. The Internet network is a large, worldwide connection of computers which have the capability of sharing information (in electronic form) at an exceptionally high speed, and with a very high degree of reliability.

An analogy related to the Internet network (which is more than a bit overused) is the system of roads and highways which allow automobile traffic throughout a geographic area. In fact, the Internet is often termed the "information highway" by many people, especially political figures and journalists, who use the expression to describe the complex telecommunications network known as the Internet.

However, if we follow that line of thinking for a moment, and envision the network of roadways and highways as analogous to the network of electronic pathways on the Internet, we can outline some of the similarities between these two types of networks. First, let's note these following characteristics about the roads and highways which allow vehicular traffic on them:

1. The vehicular highways allow access to *different types of traffic*, such as automobiles, motorcycles, pick-up trucks, motor homes, semi-tractor trailers, and buses.

2. Highways allow more than one vehicle on them at a time. (Otherwise, they wouldn't be very valuable for people to use!) Traffic flows in different lanes, while each lane has a number of vehicles following each other in succession.

3. There are main highways, such as the interstate highways in the United States, smaller highways, as in the state and county highways, and yet even smaller roadways, including the very smallest gravel roads that may service rural areas and which could pass by remote farmhouses. All these roads and highways, regardless of their size or type of construction, allow vehicular traffic to pass along them.

4. Traffic flows much *faster* on the large, main highways, which are built to handle this higher rate of flow, and which often include many "lanes" to handle a significantly higher density of traffic.

5. The larger the highway, the more "lanes" it will likely have, which allows more vehicles to travel along it at the same time (on these parallel pathways).

6. People traveling on the highways must obey the "rules of the road," or traffic accidents could occur, which would slow all the vehicles that are using that section of roadway. For example, when a car merges onto a freeway, it must wait until there is a suitable opening in the traffic to enter safely without causing a collision. Also, when cars arrive at a traffic semaphore, those at the red light must wait until the light changes before they are allowed to pass through the intersection. As another example, vehicles following other vehicles in traffic lanes must maintain a safe distance between each other, or collisions would be more likely to occur.

7. As the number of vehicles traveling on any section of roadway increases, the average speed of traffic through that section tends to decrease. At "rush hour," for example, traffic in many cities slows considerably due to the high density of traffic.

Now, let's take a look at how the Internet "highways" work in a similar fashion. Although they're not designed for the passage of motor vehicles, the Internet roadways allow electrical signals representing *information* to pass along them, effectively passing that information between various computers on the network. You will note these similarities between traffic on vehicular highways and information traveling on computer networks.

1. Different information types pass along the Internet. A file of electronic information which is traveling down the Internet highways often contains one or more of the following electronic *documents*:

   - *Textual* documents include the main contents of e-mail messages. Text-based documents are simple in form and allow only the characters of the alphabet, the digits, punctuation symbols, and a few other characters to be included. Textual documents are sometimes referred to as ASCII documents or files. ASCII (pronounced "ask-key") is an acronym for the American Standard for Character Information Interchange, which is a method for encoding typical "typewriter"-based characters in a computer. Text-based documents allow only the characters that are on the keys of a basic typewriter, both lowercase and uppercase, to be included.

     Textual (ASCII) files are valuable for conveying basic information, but they do *not* allow the inclusion of different types and sizes of **fonts,** or the use of **bold** and *italic* typefaces. Also, they do not contain "page-formatting" information such as margin sizes, page numbers, "headers and footers," and other fancy features incorporated in most word processors. In fact, modern word processors all allow the saving of documents in text-only form, which automatically removes all such formatting information from the file. In addition, graphics and pictures cannot be included in text documents, except through elaborate encoding schemes which are used for that purpose.

     ASCII-text-based documents are a very useful form of sharing information between users on the Internet because virtually all computers can read, write, and process them. Also, all printers can easily handle text files, without any additional software needed.

     [Note that since the saved form of an information document is typically a "file" in a computer system, documents on the Internet are often referred to as *files*, and the terms *document* and *file* are often used interchangeably in this context.]

- *Word processing* documents are files created with the use of word processors, and include text but also additional information related to the formatting of the document, including any fonts and type-faces used, pagination, graphics or tables, and other features typically included with modern word processors. These types of files are not encoded using the ASCII system and are referred to generally as "binary" files. The information contained in binary files can be very complex and will generally include a larger variety of information types than do ASCII text files. The following categories also represent binary files and documents.

- *Computer program* files are a very commonly found document type which exists online. Many people exchange programs through electronic file transfers, and large numbers of freely accessible programs (or programs that may be used at no charge for a trial period) are available for downloading by students at the large number of *shareware archive* sites on the Internet.

- *Graphics* files are abundantly available, including digitized photographs, drawings, charts, maps, diagrams, and other visual information capable of being viewed on the computer screen, and printed on the printer. These documents can be found in many locations throughout the Internet. Many are freely available for downloading to your own computer, and can then be added to your own documents.

  Graphics files need special software in order to be viewed, such as a dedicated graphics program, a Web browser, or a "painting" utility. Most modern computers include software for viewing and editing such digital images, and these programs can also be obtained commercially as well as at shareware sites on the Internet. For example, a file representing a satellite-based weather image of your geographic area may be downloaded from various Web sites and viewed directly on your browser or with other graphics programs you may have available.

- *Sound* files representing music, sound effects, or the recording of the human voice (to name a few examples) are also available on the Internet for sharing among users. With the large number of sound cards currently being installed in personal computers, many users are sharing these *digitized sound* files with each other on-line. A number of sites on the Internet are dedicated to the distribution of sound files to any interested Internet users who may wish to download them to their own computers.

Sound files need special software installed on the computer in order to be heard through a speaker. Such programs are usually included with the sound card hardware, but can also be obtained commercially and as shareware. Sound files are an example of multimedia documents, which are becoming exceptionally popular to integrate with computer presentations, training programs, and on World Wide Web pages.

2. Returning to our analogy comparing the Internet with automobile highways: electronic digital information traveling the larger Internet pathways flows in separate lanes. These lanes for conveying electrical traffic on a computer network are commonly referred to as *channels*.

3. Similar to vehicular highways, the Internet also has main thoroughfares for passing digital traffic rapidly. These very large highways connecting distant geographic areas on the Internet are termed *backbones*, which allow very high volumes of electronic information to travel them at exceptionally high speeds.

Moderately sized "roadways" electronically connect cities and towns to the main backbone, whereas a smaller line is analogous to the narrow gravel road which may run by a remote farmhouse in a rural area. These various small roadways of the Internet do not allow multiple lanes of traffic to flow through them or at high rates of speed. You can envision these local traffic roadways as the "on-ramps" to the larger electronic "expressways" of the Internet.

4. As with automobile highways, digital traffic passing through the Internet also must follow a well-defined set of rules of the road, or chaos would surely occur! Luckily, the scientists who engineered the Internet developed a very effective set of rules, called a *communications protocol*, which defines how information travels through this network and in what form. This "protocol," or set of rules for electronic traffic flow, is referred to as TCP/IP (transmission control protocol/internet protocol). Any electronic information which enters the Internet from a local computer system or network must first be encoded into TCP/IP form—or it won't be allowed access.

This text is not focused on the technology underlying the operation of the Internet, but a brief analogy may assist in understanding the general purpose and workings of TCP/IP. Suppose you were in a classroom trying to conduct a meeting with a large number of fellow students who are members of a club. During the meeting, many students may wish to share information or opinions with other members of the group — either individually or with the group at large. If everyone spoke at once, no one would hear or understand much in any of the conversations! Simple "rules of order" could allow the meeting to be conducted more efficiently, such as:

- Only one person may speak at a time.

- Individuals wishing to speak must raise their hand first.

- A chairperson will call on people to speak in a regular order, so that everyone has a chance to be heard.

- Long-winded individuals must keep their comments within a designated time limit.

- One-on-one conversations are to be held in a separate conference room or in "side bar" discussions.

Disagreements and arguments between two group members could be addressed in the following manner:

- Before responding to the comments by another individual, a student must paraphrase or "repeat" what was just heard *to the satisfaction of the first person*. This would help resolve misinterpretations of the communications being shared.

- A maximum time will be allowed for each subject to be discussed during the interchange.

- Individuals may *not* interrupt each other while another person is speaking.

TCP/IP defines and controls electronic communications traffic on the Internet in a similar manner. "Conversations" are held between individual computers, and each side may only "speak" up to a maximum period of time (or amount of data shared). A computer receiving a portion of a message must "repeat" a paraphrase of what was heard to the sending computer, which must verify that it was received correctly. Also, computers must "take their turn" in sending traffic over the network, or conflicts would occur. Finally, all computers wishing to send or receive information over the Internet must eventually be allowed an opportunity to do so.

3.3 Resource Sites on the Internet

In addition to its powerful communication capabilities, the Internet is certainly the largest and most readily accessible *information resource* which has ever existed. Students who gain comfort in accessing information from electronic document and data archives over the information highways have the *world* as their "virtual research library," and knowledge of how to access this library can be very beneficial to a student's success in academic, research, and personal endeavors.

Fortunately, it is exceptionally easy to use the software Internet tools which have been developed to assist individuals in locating and accessing a voluminous body of information over the Internet. This chapter will discuss how information is stored on computer servers, and how to locate and use the software tools necessary to browse and retrieve information from those remote computer systems.

Types of Information Access Sites on the Internet

Computers which are currently connected to the Internet are referred to as "sites." FTP sites are special software tools connected to a computer system which allow users to gain access remotely (through the Internet) for the purpose of accessing files and documents stored on that computer. For example, students could log on to their school's "FTP server" computer through the Internet from any location in the world, and retrieve (download) information stored on that system for their own use.

In addition, some FTP sites allow certain users to *upload* files from their own computers to be shared with others through this medium. Let's say you took a series of photographs which you electronically *scanned* into your computer at home and wished to allow other students on your campus to view them. If your school has an FTP server which allows you uploading privileges, you could log on to that server remotely (through the Internet) and send your digitized photographs to be stored on the campus computer system for access by others. Additional file types which can be easily shared through FTP include word processed documents (such as an essay, short story, research paper, poem, or the "great American novel" you wrote), computer programs, graphics, including computer art you may have created, or even music you composed and recorded on your synthesizer at home!

Many FTP sites do *not* restrict access privileges on their file systems to their local users only. *Anonymous FTP sites* allow "anyone" to log on remotely through the Internet, giving them access to certain portions of that computer's file system. These sites are termed "anonymous" because individuals do not need to have an account on the system to gain access to the publicly accessible files located there. When logging in via the Internet to an anonymous FTP site, individuals only need to type **Anonymous** when requested to enter an account name or user ID.

Not every computer connected to the Internet has the capabilities of accessing FTP sites. The computer must have installed (or be connected to yet another computer which has installed) an FTP client program, which is special software that allows the FTP server computer and the local computer to communicate with each other. "Client" and "server" programs are discussed in more detail in Section 3.7. FTP will be discussed in further depth including an analogy of this Internet resource with a worldwide accessible "virtual library" in Section 6.3.

Anonymous FTP sites allow users to browse, retrieve, and share documents in their electronic file cabinets from anywhere in the world through the Internet.

WAIS (Wide-area information system) sites are special programs installed on computer systems which allow users to search databases of information stored in their electronic file cabinets. For example, a campus library may have a catalog of its holdings stored electronically in a very large database on the campus computer system. A WAIS server will allow campus users to access the catalog, and to find books and journals of interest very conveniently and rapidly.

WAIS servers create a large "searchable electronic index" of virtually *every word* contained in *every document* stored in the database! A student who is connected via computer to a library's database through a WAIS server may easily locate the titles and authors of all books related to a topic of interest or study.

Similar to Anonymous FTP sites, many WAIS servers are connected to the Internet and allow access to their databases to the general public. This expands the coverage of their use from the local users to individuals located throughout the world! A student, for example, could log on to the Internet from school or at home, connect to a WAIS server at NASA, and search many hundreds of documents stored at that site relating to the space shuttle program.

As with other Internet tools, accessing a server requires client software to be used in order for a connection to successfully take place between the two computer systems. WAIS servers require that individuals who wish to search the main system's databases from a remote site have a WAIS client program installed on the local computers or networks.

WAIS and FTP client software is readily available from various sources, both commercially and as shareware or freeware programs, which can be downloaded from hundreds of FTP sites on the Internet. If you are connected to your campus system, however, it is very likely that such Internet client software packages have already been installed and are available for your use.

Gopher sites are special computer servers installed on systems connected to the Internet which allow users ease of access to a variety of resources and information available online. Similar to the other tools discussed, a gopher client program must be installed for an individual to use the facilities at a gopher site. As discussed previously, client software can be obtained commercially as well as downloaded from software FTP archives on the Internet (as shareware or freeware). An example of the obtaining of such programs is illustrated in Section 6.3.

Shareware is software which is meant to be "shared" with others through various means and is easily available (usually relatively inexpensively). Alternative versions of certain shareware programs (such as those which have limited features compared to the "real" version, or which can be used for only a certain "trial period") are freely available at anonymous FTP sites (see previous paragraph). *Freeware* is just as it says—*free*—which the program authors wrote and distributed without any concern for monetary gain.

Gopher has a convenient *menu interface* which allows users to browse information on the Internet very easily by selecting items from a list of options presented on the screen. Included among the menu options at most Gopher sites is access to a very powerful searching engine named *Veronica*, which allows users to very easily locate information and resources on Internet servers distributed throughout the world! A similar tool, *Archie*, is valuable for searching the anonymous FTP sites for files of interest and can often be accessed through Gopher menus. (Comic book fans may notice the relationship between the names of these tools: Archie and Veronica.) Using Archie to search for information at anonymous FTP sites is discussed in Section 6.3.

Gopher servers allow individuals convenient access to many different types of tools and facilities, including the following:

- Text and binary files

- Graphics files which can be viewed on the computer screen or printed

- Audio files, including digitized music, spoken narrations, and sound effects

- FTP, WAIS, telnet, and other gopher sites located elsewhere on the Internet

These various Internet site types, and the tools needed to access them, are discussed in more depth in Chapter 6 of this text.

Telnet is another very useful Internet resource. "Telnet servers" allow users who are not directly connected to a local computer network to gain *remote entry* via the Internet. For example, a campus computer system may allow students to log on to the network from their homes, enabling them to use the facilities of the system as if they were sitting on campus in a computer lab. As long as students have valid accounts on the system, they may use their same user names and passwords which they need when logging in directly from school.

Some telnet sites allow *public access* for use of portions of their computer system's resources to any interested individuals through an Internet connection. For example, a campus computer network may allow telnet access to information about the school, including the college catalog, admissions information, the campus e-mail phone directory, library catalogs, news bulletins, and a variety of promotional literature for attracting students.

To enter a public access telnet server, an individual doesn't need an account on the system. Typically, when logging on, it is only necessary to enter a known word, such as **guest** or **public**. Other public telnet sites make it easier yet—you only need to press the Return (or Enter) key when prompted for an account name or user ID. After logging in, clear directions are usually presented on the screen for accessing the resources available on that system. (Most systems provide user-friendly menus to select options of interest.) Examples of the use of telnet are presented in Section 6.2.

Telnet can probably be considered the most *fundamental tool* used in gaining the resources available on the Internet. It frees users from having to be tied directly to a computer system in order to access its facilities. Historically, before other Internet access tools were available on many campus computer systems (such as gopher, Veronica, Archie, WAIS, IRC, and World Wide Web client programs), many students could still gain access to these tools by "tel-netting" to other, better-equipped computer systems through the Internet and using them remotely! To this day, a student with access to a telnet client pro-gram on the local network may access valuable Internet tools and resources on other systems located throughout the world. For example, a student without access to a WAIS or Web browsing client program on a local system may use telnet to access another system which does.

World Wide Web sites are the fastest growing and most popular resource type currently available on the Internet. "Pages" of information presented on a Web site allow convenient and rapid access to a tremendous volume and variety of resources on the Internet. When browsing the Web, it is easy and painless to branch from site to site by simply selecting ("clicking on") topics of interest which are presented on the screen. This facility for surfing the Web's re-sources by following the hot links on Web pages is referred to as *hypertext* navigation.

It is simple to surf the Web's voluminous resources by using a browser pro-gram, which allows you to easily jump from page to page, while following topics that interest you. At all times, the browser remembers where you have been, so you may backtrack to previous pages you've visited at any time. Also, virtually all browsers allow you to set *bookmarks* on pages you may wish to visit at a future time.

3.4   Software Tools for Accessing Internet Sites

Computers cannot perform any function whatsoever without programs which run on them called software. A "piece of software," a "software package," and a "software system" all refer to computer programs which have been written (and are "*run*") for the purpose of accomplishing tasks with a computer sys-tem. Internet communications and resource-providing sites all need software to accomplish their intended function.

This text will continue to emphasize the Web (Internet) browser as the tool of choice for accessing a large variety of Internet resources in an exceptionally convenient way. Browsers have the capability of easily navigat-ing the user between Web pages, FTP sites, telnet servers, WAIS database re-trieval sites, and gopher menu-based access sites.

3.5 Internet Site Names and Addresses

Each computer site on the Internet must have a unique identifying number called an *IP address* in order for it to be installed for use on the Internet. Analogous to the way vehicles on the motor highways must have registration numbers or license plates easily distinguishable to others on the road, every Internet site which is sending or receiving information must have a unique IP address stamped on it.

IP (*Internet protocol*) addresses all have the same form: each is a series of four numbers separated by three periods, such as {123.216.78.90} or {45.132.73.54}. One stipulation is that each number in the four groups must be *less than 256*. Each number corresponds to a region of the world where the Internet site is located, going from the general region to specific subregions as you move from left to right in the number sequence.

When a student is using a computer to log on to the Internet, that computer must have a unique IP address assigned to it. If that computer is part of a local network, such as in a campus computer lab, the numbers are assigned by the central computers which are controlling the operation of the network. If you are connected to the Internet through a modem, a number (often only temporarily, while you are online) is assigned to your computer for the duration of the time you're connected.

All servers on the Internet also have IP addresses assigned to them, and it is necessary for a client program (such as an e-mailing program) to know the address of the user's mail server computer in order to successfully connect with it and exchange communications. For example, if you are surfing the Web with a browser program, and you select a "hot link" on the screen, the browser will first need to look up the IP address of the Web page you have selected to visit before it can successfully branch to that server's location (site).

Site Addresses May Be Associated with *Names*

Since numbers aren't always easy for human beings to remember, software tools were developed which allow *names* to be assigned to IP addresses. For example, a popular shareware FTP site where Internet users can download programs is located at the IP address 134.228.45.0, but that address has been assigned the name ftp.coast.net. An FTP client program running on your computer may connect with this FTP site by knowing either its IP address—such as 134.228.45.0—or the site name assigned to this IP address, such as 134.228.45.0—or the site name assigned to this IP address, ftp.coast.net.

If the second method is used, a client program must first look up the name ftp.coast.net in the electronic "address books" of the Internet in order to find its actual IP address, 134.228.45.0. Special-purpose computer servers connected to the Internet (called *name servers*) are used by client programs for this purpose.

When a client program needs to find an address, it connects to a name server computer on the Internet and submits a "site name" to it (such as ftp.coast.net). This server computer will then check its electronic address book for the name submitted by the client program. If the name is in its database, it will return to the client the IP address requested. If it is not successful, it will then connect with other name server computers on the Internet for help in locating the correct address submitted by the client.

If this is all starting to seem a bit complicated, let's try an analogy to describe this process. Suppose you needed to locate the telephone number of a friend who moved recently. You could try calling the local telephone company for directory assistance to obtain the number, and you would speak with an operator who would look up the name of the person in a local telephone directory. If this doesn't successfully locate the number, you may have to dial to a long-distance directory service. In that case, the operator may scan directories from various other cities in attempting to look up your friend's name.

Name server computers operate in a similar way. If the site name is not available in the local directory, that computer will check with other directory services (by contacting other name servers on the Internet). Luckily, this process is all done automatically ("behind the scenes") for you, the user. When you enter a site name to a client application, such as a mailing, FTP, telnet, or Web browsing program, you will usually be connected to the site without any problems. However, on some occasions, name server computers go down, and you may not succeed in connecting to the site you wish to explore. In that case, you may need to enter the actual IP address to connect successfully, or wait until another time when the servers are operating correctly.

In summary, all Internet sites (computers currently connected to the Internet) need an IP address in the form of [#.#.#.#] (where each # stands for a number less than 256). A *site name* may be "registered" so that it is entered into the various databases used by the name servers on the Internet. It's the responsibility of these name server computers to look up site names and return to their clients the correct IP addresses for the names requested.

3.6   Uniform Resource Locators (URLs)

When accessed through a World Wide Web browser, sites are given special names called *uniform resource locators* (URLs). A URL is an alternative address of a site on the Internet which describes:

1. The *type* of site it is (for example, Web page, gopher, FTP site, telnet).

2. The *name* of the site (including its domain and the name of the machine or network). Some large systems have "subdomains" and "subnetworks," so URLs can be quite lengthy.

3. Which *file directory* to access when you connect with the site.

4. The *name of the file* or document of interest.

URL addresses are needed by Web browsing programs to access sites on the Internet. Sometimes, these addresses are very long and can seem quite cryptic in appearance. For example, the financial aid resource page on a Web page is located at the URL address

   http://www.ed.gov/prog_info/SFA/StudentGuide/1996-97/index.html

Let's break this address down into identifiable components.

*   http:// indicates the *type* of Internet site being referenced by the browser, in this example a Web page ("http" is an abbreviation for a *hypertext document*). Documents at FTP sites begin with ftp://, gopher sites with gopher://, and telnet sites with telnet://, for example. Other URL prefixes frequently seen on Web pages indicating other types of Internet sites include

     news: *News server* sites

     mailto: E-mail addresses of Internet users

*   www.ed.gov is the name assigned to the main IP address for this site, which belongs to the U.S. Department of Education. As discussed in the preceding section, sites on the Internet can be assigned *names* which reference the actual IP address of the site. This is also referred to as the *domain*, which is the name assigned to the site. In this example, we can further break down the domain www.ed.gov (from right to left) into the following parts:

     www.ed.<u>gov</u> refers to the *class* of site, (such as government sponsored, educational, commercial, military, or location in a country other than the United States). This example is a U.S. government-based site, as denoted by the .gov abbreviation. Educational sites have domain names ending with the suffix .edu, military with .mil, commercial sites with .com; and countries can include a variety of abbreviations, such as .ca—Canada, .dk—Denmark, .au—Australia, and .uk—the United Kingdom.

www.<u>ed</u>.gov refers to the *name* of the institution or organization which is "hosting" the Internet site. In this example, .ed is an abbreviation for the U.S. Department of Education.

<u>www</u>.ed.gov denotes the *type* of computer server being accessed at a site. Web site domain names often—*but not always*—begin with www., whereas FTP server domains usually begin with ftp.

- /prog_info/SFA/StudentGuide/1996-97/index.html refers to the name of the document being accessed at the site (index.html)—along with the file directory in which it is located (/prog_info/SFA/StudentGuide/1996-97/). File directories on Web servers are arranged for access in a "treelike" fashion. Each / symbol denotes a *subdirectory*, or "branch" in the directory tree.

Students new to computer filing systems may be confused at this point. However, it isn't crucial for the Internet user to understand the details of how computer servers arrange files and documents in their electronic file cabinets. Suffice it to say that files are organized by category in electronic file folders called directories, which themselves can be contained within larger directories, and so forth. This method of organizing huge quantities of information by forming categories and subcategories for convenient access is commonly used in electronic filing systems.

In this example, the main document entitled index.html is in the

1996-97/ directory, which is a subdirectory contained in the

StudentGuide/ directory, a subdirectory contained in the

SFA/ directory contained in the

prog_info/ directory—in the "root" file directory on this server.

- http://wuarchive.wustl.edu is the name of a Web page (the prefix http:// informs me that it is a hypertext or Web document).

  In addition, the wustl.edu domain indicates an educational institution (an abbreviated name for Washington University).

- ftp://ftp.coast.net/mirrors/ is an FTP site, with the domain name coast.net, and specifying the mirrors subdirectory.

- telnet://hollis.harvard.edu is a telnet site (harvard.edu is the domain name for Harvard University; hollis is the name assigned by Harvard to this telnet computer server).

- gopher://blick.journ.latech.edu/ refers to an educational gopher site.

- news://misc.writing is the URL for the misc.writing newsgroup.

3.7   Internet Client and Server Software Tools

When a user logs on to the Internet to gather information from a remote server computer, the two computers will establish communications and begin a conversation with each other to make that information transfer happen successfully.

The program running on the computer which is requesting information is called the client program (or client, for short), and the computer program which attempts to provide that information to the client is known as the server. Note that it is the computer programs, or software, running on each respective computer that are actually controlling the whole process and allowing the conversation to happen.

As a typical example, an FTP server program running on an FTP server computer on the Internet allows a client computer to download files from the server's file archives. To repeat: *it is the computer programs, or software, running on the client and server computers that are controlling the transfer of information between the two.* The user of the Internet who wishes to download files from document archives using FTP must have direct or indirect access to an FTP client program to connect successfully. Similarly, a computer on the Internet which is to be used as an FTP server needs an FTP server program running on its computer system.

When the client and server programs are running on the two computers, they may connect and enter into a conversation with each other, allowing the FTP processes for information transfer between the client and server computers to occur. Incidentally, the technology of information transfer between clients and servers is known as (what else?) *client–server technology*, which is the basis of all information transfer and electronic communications on the Internet.

One function of the client and server software is to encode and decode information transferred through the Internet from (or into) TCP/IP form (which is discussed in Section 3.2). This TCP/IP software is responsible for breaking up files transmitted over the Internet into a stream of small "envelopes" of data called *packets*. Packets of electronic information are sent one at a time from the client site to the server, and vice versa, during a conversation between the two.

Each single packet that travels the Internet is verified for accuracy when it arrives at its destination. The individual packets which make up a file are reassembled after reaching the destination computer. Breaking a file into packets allows the TCP/IP software to perform "error checking," so that information is communicated *reliably* between the sending and receiving computers.

This text is not geared toward the technology which drives the Internet, but it is easy to understand one reason why electronic data is passed through the Internet in packet form to ensure accuracy in communications. Suppose you were passing along a large piece of information to a friend over the telephone, such as a long list of names and telephone numbers. Rather than giving your friend all the numbers on the list at once, it would probably be more efficient to say only one number at a time, while requesting that your friend repeat to you what was heard.

With this "repeat it until they get it right" approach, if a number is not received by the listener correctly, the sender will continue to repeat the number—until it has been communicated accurately. If this process is continued for all numbers in the list (continuously verifying that each number sent has been received correctly), the errors in communication can be reduced considerably. Packets of electronic-based information passed through the Internet are also verified for accuracy, which allows for exceptional reliability in this form of electronic communications.

If you consider each packet traveling the Internet to be an envelope of information sent in electronic form, the IP address of the recipient is stamped on the outside of this envelope. This ensures that it will arrive at the correct destination. (IP addresses are explained in Section 3.5.)

A Mythical Conversation Between a Client and a Server

With these introductory points in mind, let's describe a conversation between a client computer and an FTP server computer on the Internet, along with some commentary provided by the author (in italics) as to what the two computers are really "thinking" about while the conversation is taking place. Please keep in mind that computer programs really do not think, but we can at least *imagine* what they might say if they did.

In this rather strange "virtual discussion," the FTP server program is having a bit of a bad day, as you will soon see. Note that the client program is requesting a download of a computer graphics file of a picture of Hawaii. Let's listen in.

Client: [Dials the server's address on the Internet "phone line"]

Server: [Answers] Yes, this is server 123.156.78.90, what can I do for you?

Client: This is an FTP client at address 142.54.23.192. I'd like to request a download of a document from your collection. [*I sure hope I can get on the server today, and get this picture of a windsurfing beach!*]

Server: Yes, client 142.54.23.192, I've received your request for a connection. [*Oh no! Not another client request! Here I was hoping client requests were going to calm down for awhile; I'm already servicing 385 requests right now, and a few more thousand before the end of the hour!*]

Client: May I connect with you? [*I hope the server isn't too busy today.*]

Server: Yes, you're connected. [*Just tell me what you want, I'm busy here.*]

Client: I'd like to download the file "hawaii99.jpg" if I may. [*I can't afford to go to Hawaii, so I may as well look at a picture of it.*]

Server: OK, hang on. Locating file "hawaii99.jpg" [*Oh no, now I have to get that large graphics file, make a copy of it, and send it to my "packet man" to break it up into chunks. . . . I need a new way to make a living!*]

Client: OK. [*I hope this won't take too long . . . the Internet seems busier than usual today.*]

Server: OK, ready to send all the packets for file: "hawaii99.jpg" on this end; are you ready to receive? [*He better be ready to receive, or I'll time out his connection and "shut him down" for wasting my valuable time!*]

Client: Wait, please. [*Oh no, my computer has a mail client program getting some packets for a message from my "mail server." It might delay us a couple of seconds here. . . . I hope "Mr. Server" doesn't get too angry at me. . . .*]

Server: OK, waiting. [*You're telling ME to wait? . . . I've got about 400 other clients requesting information, and 72,658,639 packets en route to destinations all over the Internet, and you're telling ME to WAIT??!*]

Client: Ready to receive. [*I sure wish I was the ONLY client program running on this student's computer. I hate to make these servers wait; they have such big egos!*]

Server: OK, beginning to transmit packets. [*It's about time, "Mr. Big Shot" client wasting my valuable time . . . making me wait. . . !*]

[. . . After a few seconds. . . .]

Client: Packet #463 is corrupted; please resend it!

Server: OK, resending Packet #463. [*I'm tired of resending all these packets over the lousy phone lines some of these clients use. I swear I'm going to start charging them for all those lost packets I have to resend all the time. . . .*]

[. . . A little while later. . . .]

Client: Packet #463 received OK.

Server: OK. Continuing to send remaining packets.

[. . . A little while later. . . .]

Client: Packet #2785 is invalid; please resend it! [*I wish things would go faster on this Internet sometimes; maybe it's time to buy a faster modem. . . .*]

Server: OK, resending Packet #2785. [*I hate transmission errors; they make me work too hard. . . .*]

[. . . A little while later. . . .]

Client: Packet #2785 received OK.

Server: OK. Continuing to send remaining packets. [*Twenty-four hours a day I download files to these clients, and never ONCE has a single client computer thanked me!*]

[. . . A little while later. . . .]

Client: Last packet received—counting total packets received.

Server: OK. [*Hurry up, will you please?! I'm in the process of sending files to clients all over the world here!*]

Client: Total of 8354 packets received intact. Verify please.

Server: OK, that checks with 8354 packets sent on this end. [*I wonder when it will be time for MY vacation to Maui??*]

Client: All packets received OK. [*Now all I have to do is assemble all these packets into the right order, strip off the excess information, store it all into a file on this student's disk, and I can do something else for a while!*]

Server: OK. Any other requests? [*I sure hope not, I'm getting tired of this client computer and that stupid Hawaii picture. . . .*]

Client: Not today. Preparing to disconnect.

Server: OK. [*Thank goodness that guy is leaving! Now I have only the other 485,000 clients that will request information from me today, and I'm finished . . . until I start again tomorrow!*]

Client: Client 142.54.23.192 disconnecting. . . .

Server: Connection closed! [*Good riddance! Sure hope you appreciate all the work I did for you giving you that picture of the Maui coastline.*]

Summary

A common analogy for the Internet is the system of roads and highways that vehicles travel on. The Internet is often called the information highway, although information highways would be a more correct expression.

Main highways can pass more traffic, at a faster rate, than the smaller roads. High-speed routes on the Internet are known as backbones.

As larger highways have multiple lanes to handle more traffic, high-speed Internet connections contain space for multiple channels of information flow.

Analogous to the rules of the road of the motor vehicle highways, the protocol which governs all Internet traffic and information transfer is called TCP/IP.

The basic document type on the Internet is the text (ASCII) document, which consists of the standard typewriter characters, digits, and punctuation symbols only. E-mail documents are text documents. Text documents can be conveyed very efficiently through the Internet.

Other document types (called binary documents) include word processing, graphics, sound, and computer software files.

Client–server technology is the basic mechanism for all information transfer and communication over the Internet.

Servers can process requests from many clients at once, and multiple client programs can be running on a client computer at the same time. The TCP/IP protocol is responsible for controlling all this complex traffic on the Internet.

All sites on the Internet have unique IP addresses. Each address is a series of four numbers separated by periods.

Sites can be given names, which can be registered with name server computers. Client programs can access sites by name when the site has been registered in the name server's address book.

Review Questions

1. What defines the rules of the road for information traveling on the Internet?

2. What is the name for the superhighways of the Internet?

3. Why is information which is transferred along the Internet first broken into "packets"?

4. What information is stamped on each packet which is traveling the Internet to a destination?

5. What types of information are *not* included in ASCII text documents?

6. What tools are often needed to display graphics files on the display screen?

7. Describe some examples of multimedia documents which currently exist on the Internet.

8. Describe some nontextual (*binary*) document types on the Internet.

9. Explain the function of software client and server programs.

10. What is the format of all Internet IP addresses?

11. Describe the function of a name server.

12. How are Internet site names registered on the Internet?

13. List the URL prefix for the following types of sites on the Internet:

    Hypertext—HTML

    Gopher

    FTP

    Telnet

    Newsgroups

    E-mail addresses

Exercise

1. Summarize the following site types on the Internet for their purpose, tools needed to access them, and their URL prefix:

   FTP

   Telnet

   Gopher

   WWW (Web)

   Newsgroups

Chapter 4

The World Wide Web

4.1   Overview

This chapter will present the World Wide Web network of resources and tools. A description of hypertext is followed by the use of Web browsers. Using bookmarks for storing pages on the Web for future reference is recommended and discussed. Searching the Web with engines designed for that purpose is also emphasized.

Following the introductory section is an integrated online.tour with the College Success Web Page, located at the URL:

http://www.luminet.net/~jackp/success.htm

If you have Web access, and even minimal browser skills, I encourage you to log on to the Internet, launch your browser, and surf along with us as we explore the Web's depth and breadth of resources related to the needs of college students. Click or select CONTENTS to reach the Web links related to the illustrations in this text.

At the bottom of some of the pages, beneath the "screen shot vista" for a site being explored, is an encouragement to use a Web search engine to explore related online resources. As the Web changes and evolves, site names and addresses will change or disappear entirely. The student must be knowledgeable in finding new information and resources in the future.

So gentlemen and gentlewomen,

Start your browser engines!

4.2   Welcome to the Web

The best way to start learning about the Web is to get on the Web and start exploring it. If you have access to the Internet and a WWW client program, such as Netscape's Navigator browser, Internet Explorer by Microsoft, or the Lynx (text-based Web access) program, "start it up" and explore along with us as we tour Web pages and research valuable Internet resources for students. Let's start our Web tour at the *Student Survival Guide* online manual dedicated to new and returning college students (Figure 4.1). This "hyperbook" allows the student to explore many Internet resources directly by simply clicking on the hyperlinks on the screen. Below the caption in each figure shown is the Web address (URL) to enter into your browser. *Please note that the pages you see online may be different from those illustrated, as the Web is in constant evolution.*

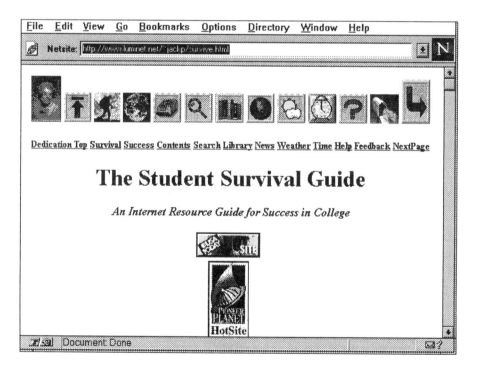

Fig. 4.1 An online *Student Survival Guide* for college students

http://www.luminet.net/~jackp/success.htm#fig4-1

Hypertext Links to Other Web Pages and Internet Resources

A Web page is a visual medium. Note in Figure 4.2 that the small pictures ("icons") on the top of screens are "clickable," meaning they are direct *links* to other Internet resources, which could be located anywhere in the world. Words which appear underlined or emphasized (when using many browsers) are hyperlinks to other pages at the current Web site, or to sites elsewhere on the Internet. Clicking your mouse on a hyperlink will instruct your Web browser to attempt to connect to the site you have selected. If you are using a text-only browser (such as Lynx), you may select a link by using designated keys (such as the arrow or Tab keys, followed by Return). Usually, directions are included on the screen or through accessible menus.

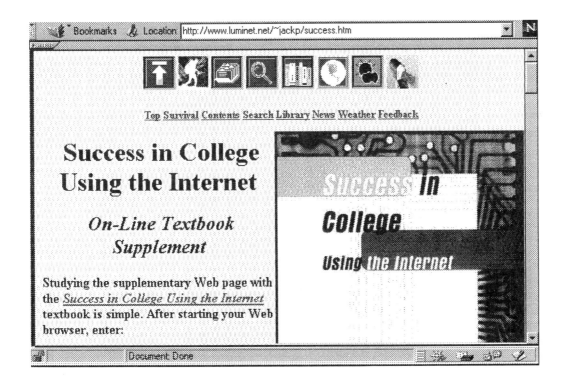

Fig. 4.2 *Success in College Using the Internet* **on the Internet**

http://www.luminet.net/~jackp/success.htm

4.3   Early Beginnings of Hypertext and the Web

It all started with Ted Nelson. His book *Computer Lib/Dream Machines* (Mindful Press) describes a method for exploring information in a "nonlinear" fashion. Nonlinear, or hypertext, presentation allows users to choose how they will explore resources at their disposal. Nelson's concept allowed readers to follow associations between ideas, rather than simply proceed through the resources in a sequential fashion. Imagine a book with pages that have special "hot spot" links on them. If the reader decides to explore a hyperlink subject in more detail, simply pointing a finger at that spot on the page causes that book (or a different one) to immediately open to the correct page! Replace the "finger" with a mouse, and you have online hypertext with a modern browsing program.

4.4   What Is the World Wide Web?

The World Wide Web (WWW) was developed by Tim Berners-Lee at the European Center for Particle Physics—CERN, in Geneva, Switzerland (Figure 4.3). His idea was to develop a means for efficiently sharing information among geographically dispersed physics researchers. He incorporated a means for navigating the resources of the Internet using the hypertext methods devised by Ted Nelson. Web pages of information can be viewed in text form only, using text browsers such as Lynx, though this text will emphasize graphic-based browsers, which can present multimedia resources as well as text. Areas on Web pages that are highlighted are often linked to other Internet resources and can reference Web pages, gopher, FTP, and telnet sites.

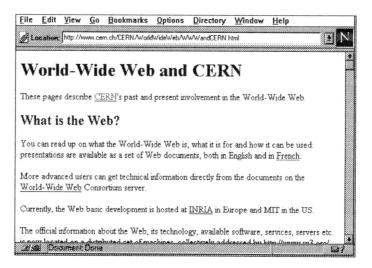

Fig. 4.3 The birthplace of the World Wide Web at CERN

http://www.luminet.net/~jackp/success.htm#fig4-3

Following Hypertext Links Through the Web

After selecting the Help option in the *Student Survival Guide* screen shown on page 70 (or by clicking on the "question mark" button), I am presented with the screen shown in Figure 4.4, which documents the meaning of the various small pictures or icons on the pages of this online book. The ability to quickly jump from one Web page to another on the Internet makes surfing these worldwide electronic resources an easy task. All browsers have the capability to back up to previous screens. Explore the Back option on your browser, as you may use it often. If you reach a site that you want to visit again in the future, be sure to add a *bookmark* for that page and you will then be able to easily access it in the future. A menu option is available on modern browsers for editing bookmark links or "favorites."

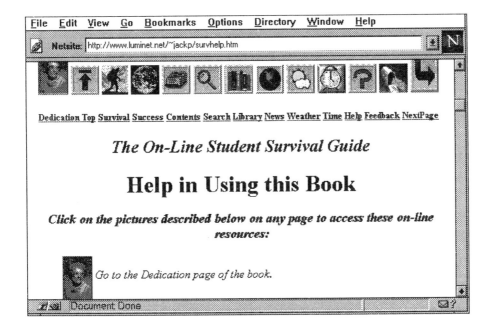

Fig. 4.4 Graphics hyperlinks on a Web page

http://www.luminet.net/~jackp/success.htm#fig4-4

4.5   Setting Bookmarks with Your Browser

If you visit a site which you wish to return to at another session, set a bookmark to keep it on a list for future reference. Most Web browsers allow saving bookmarks, and bookmark categories, to allow users to store Web page titles and URLs for future reference. Experienced surfers of the Web tend to develop very comprehensive and well-indexed *bookmark files,* which allow them to return to sites of interest quickly and conveniently (Figure 4.5). *If you are a user of a computer shared by others, you may not be able to save personal bookmarks.*

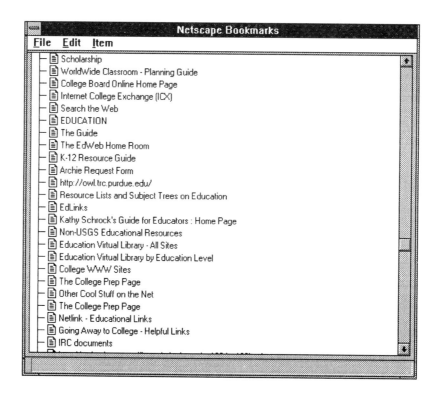

Fig. 4.5   Editing a bookmark file in a Web browser

Example: Weather Forecasts Through the Web

The Internet has many weather forecasting pages available through the Web which provide up-to-the-hour weather forecasts (Figure 4.6). By entering the name of a city, I can receive a current weather forecast for a particular region of the country, as well as an extended forecast.

Many different Web sites sponsor weather-related pages for interested Internet users. Those students using browsers with graphics capabilities can view satellite image maps of weather conditions throughout the world.

Fig. 4.6 A Web page dedicated to weather information

http://www.luminet.net/~jackp/success.htm#fig4-6

4.6   Using the Web Search Engines

Finding information on the Internet and Web is greatly simplified with the development of huge database search engines developed for that purpose. *Alta-Vista* (by Digital Equipment Corp.) is a very powerful engine which has literally millions of Web pages indexed by practically every word in every document of all pages accessible on the Web (Figure 4.7). Using a search engine is simple: type in a keyword or two, click Submit, and let the engine do the rest of the work. *AltaVista* will search the entire Web and return to you a list of pages which best match the words you entered. Clicking on a page entry shown on the list will direct your browser to connect you immediately to that Web server and load the page requested.

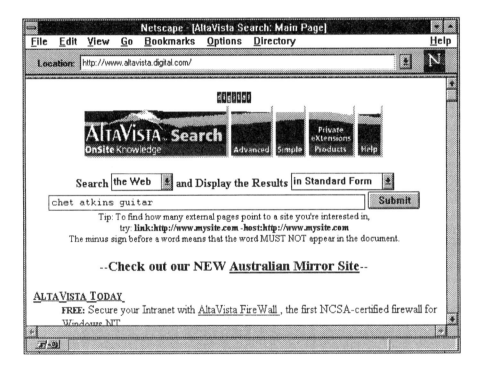

Fig. 4.7 The *AltaVista* search engine page on the Web

http://www.luminet.net/~jackp/success.htm#fig4-7

Reproduced with the permission of Digital Equipment Corporation. AltaVista and the AltaVista logo and the Digital logo are trademarks of Digital Equipment Corporation.

Additional Searching Tools on the Web

A large number of search engines for locating information on the Internet currently exist, and many more are being developed. Finding information in such a vast virtual library of information would be a difficult task without such powerful tools. Figure 4.8 shows links to many facilities on the Web for finding resources of interest.

Note that not all searching tools operate identically. Most of the engines, however, do include a Help screen for assisting users in their searches. Also, some tools will search the World Wide Web and the Usenet newsgroups depending on the option chosen. A newsgroup search will find articles posted to Usenet which relate to the keywords entered by the user.

Fig. 4.8 Links to Internet Searching Engines

http://www.luminet.net/~jackp/success.htm#fig4-8

4.7   Using an Index to Find Resources on the Web

In addition to the keyword search engines illustrated on the previous pages, large lists (indices) of Web pages are kept at various virtual libraries on the Web. Many times the provider of a Web index has invested a considerable amount of time and energy to keep that index current. (The Web is a very dynamic medium, and Web site addresses frequently change.) An excellent example of a very comprehensive index (and one of the most useful sites on the Internet) is the *Yahoo* "general index" to the Web and Internet (Figure 4.9). Web pages are categorized in a very easy-to-browse fashion, and a searching facility is also included.

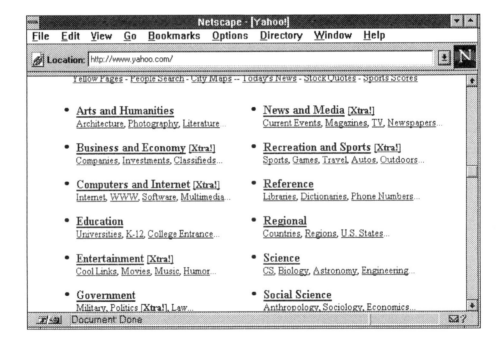

Fig. 4.9 Categories and subcategories in the *Yahoo* index

http://www.yahoo.com

Text and artwork copyright © 1996 by YAHOO!, INC. All rights reserved.
YAHOO! and the YAHOO! logo are trademarks of YAHOO!, Inc.

4.8   How Hypertext Links Use Site URL Addresses

Remember that all sites on the Internet, *when accessed from a Web page*, are given special addresses called uniform resource locators (URLs). Your browser will usually have the current URL of the page you are viewing listed in a line near the top of the screen.

Figure 4.10 shows a Web page designed to include a graphic (picture) link so the user can directly branch to a specific page at the *Yahoo* index.

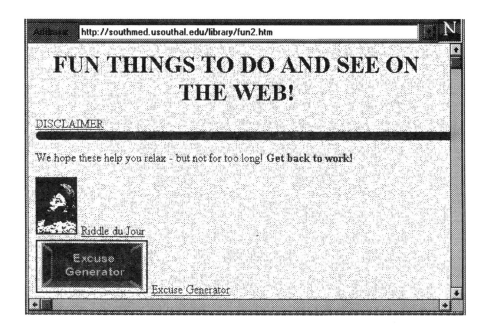

Fig. 4.10 An index of fun places to explore on the Web

http://www.luminet.net/~jackp/success.htm#fig4-10

4.9 Financial Aid Resources for Students

Online financial aid resources for students are an important contribution of the Internet's electronic communication and information-sharing capabilities. Many individuals and organizations (Figure 4.11) have constructed Web pages which index a huge variety of documents related to college financial aid.

Hint: To speed up the time it takes to load pages, turn the graphics to off by selecting that option from your browser menu. The information is presented without pictures displayed (in text-only form) but much more rapidly! Some pages, however, use graphics to display menus or links to other pages—so graphics must be switched to on in these cases.

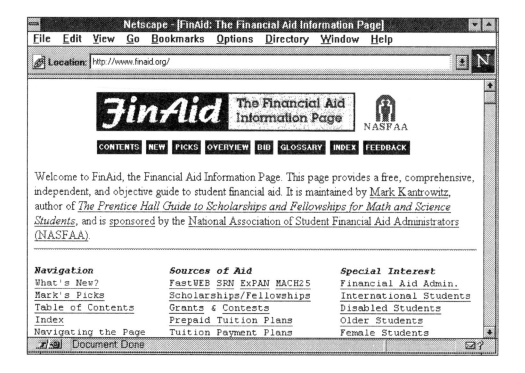

Fig. 4.11 A page of links to student financial aid resources

http://www.luminet.net/~jackp/success.htm#fig4-11

Searching for Scholarships Online

Scholarship and grant information for students is plentiful on the Web. Those pursuing graduate or professional schools have access to fellowship resources provided by many organizations.

The page shown in Figure 4.12 is dedicated to providing financial aid and scholarship searching resources for students. Note that some of the organizations which provide scholarship-searching capabilities charge a fee! *Read the screens carefully.*

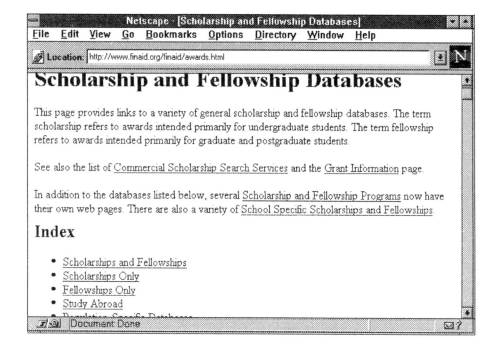

Fig. 4.12 Researching scholarships and fellowships online

http://www.luminet.net/~jackp/success.htm#fig4-12

A Map to Universities in the United States

University Pages has a nice Web page which uses a colorful map graphic to allow the user to search for a university by selecting a state on the map with the mouse (Figure 4.13). When I visited the page, I clicked on the state of Oregon, and it displayed a list of all four-year colleges and universities in that state. When selecting a university on the list (I chose the University of Oregon), I was branched to the "homepage" of that institution.

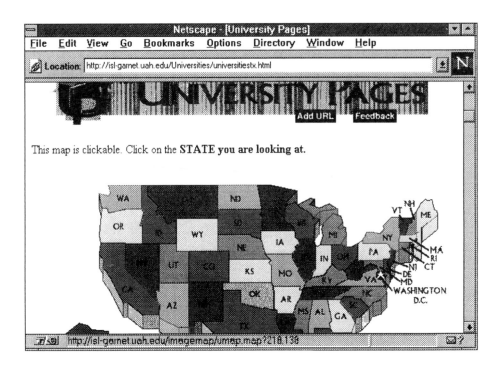

Fig. 4.13 A map interface to universities in the United States

http://www.luminet.net/~jackp/success.htm#fig4-13

University of Oregon Homepage on the Web

The University of Oregon's *homepage* on the Web (Figure 4.14) is an example of a Campus Wide Information System (CWIS). Online campus resources available from this page include admissions information for prospective students, access to the campus phone book, a school calendar of events, faculty research interests, and alumni news — in addition to a wealth of other campus resources.

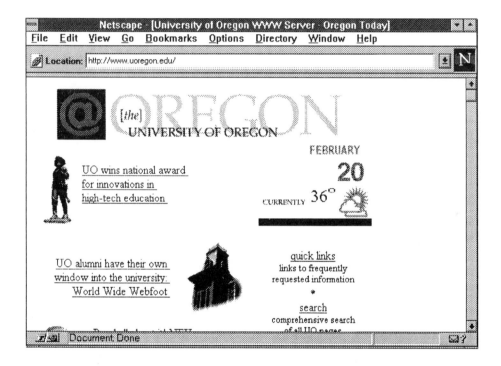

Fig. 4.14 University of Oregon's homepage on the Web

http://www.luminet.net/~jackp/success.htm#fig4-14

Reprinted by permission of the University of Oregon. Copyright 1996.

Honolulu Community College Homepage

The Honolulu Community College homepage (Figure 4.15) is an excellent example of the use of the Web to distribute information about a school to the world community. Included on these Campus Wide Information System pages are many links to campus resources. *Take some time to explore the pages at your own college's Web site.* Many schools now publish their entire college bulletin online, as well as other resources such as the library catalog and journal index, registration information and class schedules, admissions information, financial aid resources, the campus newspaper, and events calendars.

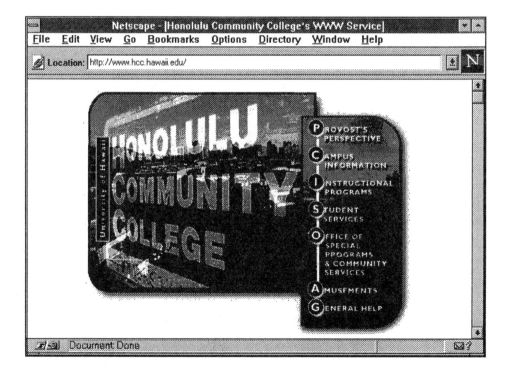

Fig. 4.15 Honolulu Community College's WWW page

http://www.luminet.net/~jackp/success.htm#fig4-15

An Interactive Online Campus Map

From the homepage of Honolulu Community College, a click of the mouse brings you to an interactive map of the campus (Figure 4.16). Click on the area of the college you would like to explore, and you will be branched immediately to a Web page corresponding to the area you selected. Interactive maps are a powerful, visual-based searching tool and are used extensively on the Web. *Turn graphics to on using the Options menu on pages that use maps or pictures extensively for navigating the Web site.*

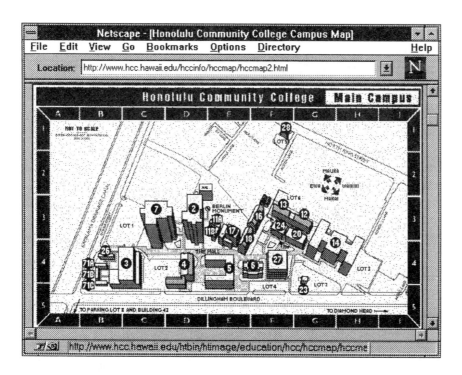

Fig. 4.16 A clickable map of Honolulu Community College

http://www.luminet.net/~jackp/success.htm#fig4-16

4.10   Online Books, Magazines, Journals, and Newspapers

Electronic versions of magazines, journals, and newspapers are being offered online in large numbers through the Internet. A student wishing to learn up-to-date information about another country or culture may wish to read the latest news "straight from the source" in an online edition of a foreign newspaper. Also, electronic versions of academic journals are published with increasing frequency on the Internet. Figure 4.17 presents an index of online scholarly *electronic journals* ("e-journals") available for reading on the Web.

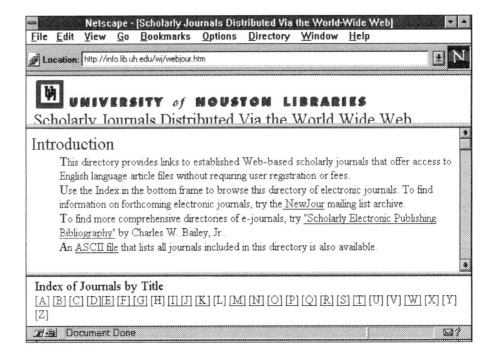

Fig. 4.17 An index to scholarly electronic journals

http://www.luminet.net/~jackp/success.htm#fig4-17

E-Zines: Electronic Online Magazines

Figure 4.18 shows an online "e-zine" distributed through the Internet (this particular example is sent to users via e-mail). Thousands of *electronic magazines* are being distributed in a very cost-effective fashion to interested readers worldwide. Sometimes, e-zines are distributed at Web or gopher sites, whereas others are sent to subscribers through regular e-mail. Recent developments and late-breaking news in many areas of knowledge can be accessed over the Internet by subscribing (often at no cost whatsoever) to these online publications.

Fig. 4.18 An online e-zine distributed through the Internet

http://www.luminet.net/~jackp/success.htm#fig4-18

4.11 Virtual Libraries and Indexes to Web Resources

Many Web sites, such as the page at Rutgers University shown in Figure 4.19, maintain a comprehensive index of a large number of online reference books and informational materials of value to students. Electronic versions of reference materials accessible through this page include dictionaries, encyclopedias, almanacs, biographies, consumer guides, calendars, college and graduate school directories, atlases, geography books, grants and scholarships listings, medical information, and style manuals. *The search engine pages and virtual library pages are the most important research resources available for students to gain facility on the Web.*

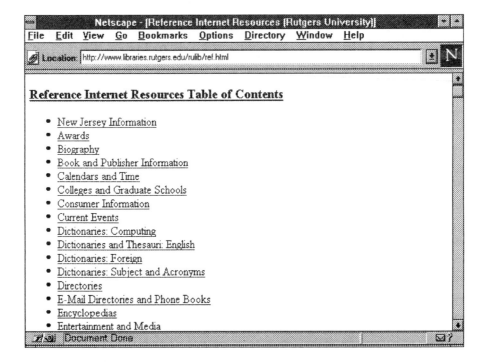

Fig. 4.19 A comprehensive index to online reference materials

http://www.luminet.net/~jackp/success.htm#fig4-19

Education Resources in a Virtual Library

Stetson University has a very well-designed virtual library on the Web that is illustrated in Figure 4.20. Educational resource links in this online library include a tutorial on the Internet, search engines, tools for locating Internet e-mail addresses, library catalogs, reference books online, government-related resources, employment information, grants, and general subject indexes for business, the humanities, the sciences, and so on.

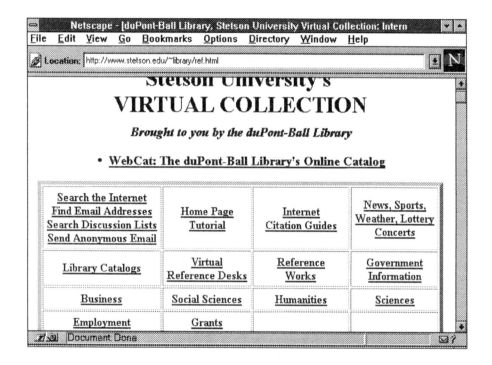

Fig. 4.20 A page of Internet resources for students of all ages

http://www.luminet.net/~jackp/success.htm#fig4-20

A Comprehensive Index of Internet Resources

One more example of an excellent index to valuable Internet resources for Internet users resides at GMI's comprehensive page (Figure 4.21). Included on this excellent site are links to current affairs, business, computers, economics, educational research, electronic books, personal finance, ethnic interests, humor, literature, online magazines and newspapers, medicine, music, performing arts, politics, science, sports, travel, U.S. government, and weather-related pages.

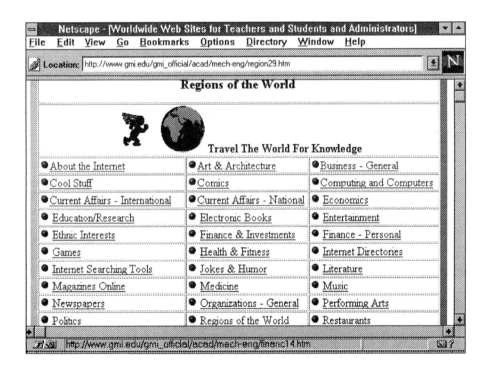

Fig. 4.21 Yet another virtual library of resources of all types

http://www.iuminet.net/~jackp/success.htm#fig4-21

By permission of GMI Engineering and Management Institute.

The World Wide Web Virtual Library

Virtual libraries, as discussed previously, are often very comprehensive indexes to large repositories of information distributed throughout the Internet and World Wide Web. The *World Wide Web Virtual Library* (WWWVL) page shown in Figure 4.22 includes references to popular areas of user interest in the library, as well as a link to a subject index and instructive information on publishing your own resources in this online information repository.

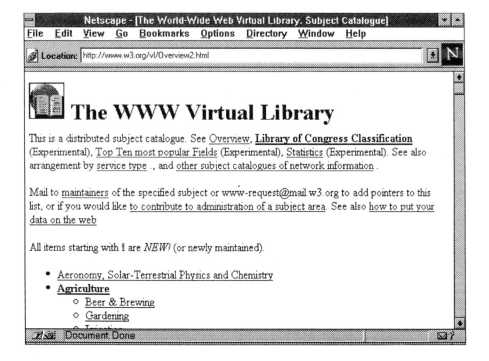

Fig. 4.22 The *World Wide Web Virtual Library* (WWWVL) subject catalog

http://www.luminet.net/~jackp/success.htm#fig4-22

An Online Lecture Hall

Online tutorials are presented, and courses are delivered, in a large number of knowledge areas through the facilities of the Internet. An excellent page to explore for information regarding online instruction in a comprehensive listing of subject areas is presented on the *World Lecture Hall* page (Figure 4.23), developed at the University of Texas. Many instructors who have written instructional materials for their own classes have made these materials available to the entire Internet community.

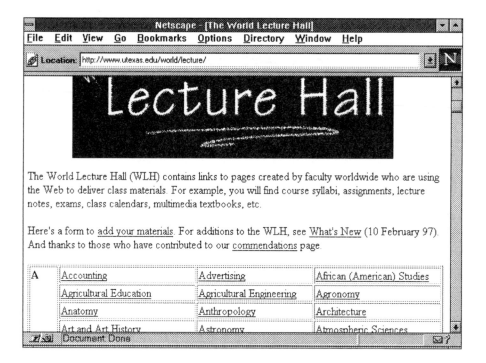

Fig. 4.23 Online courses delivered worldwide via the Web

http://www.luminet.net/~jackp/success.htm#fig4-23

A Web Page Dedicated to Women's Resources

The page shown in Figure 4.24 is dedicated to Internet resources for women. It includes a listing of the "best" sites on the Web for women, as well as a page dedicated to nineteenth-century female writers, a women-oriented business page, several indexes to other Internet-based women's resources, information about women in film, an online birth center page, "virtual sisterhood" (a global online women's support network), many pages of women's health issues, and an online chat facility.

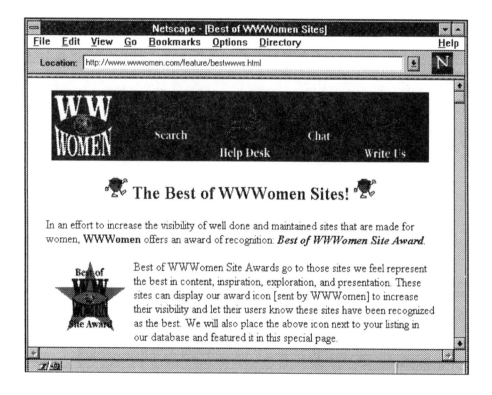

Fig. 4.24 A page of Web resources targeted for women

http://www.luminet.net/~jackp/success.htm#fig4-24

How to Design a Web Page of Your Own

Many students are interested in putting up their own Web pages, and the Internet has many available online resources for gaining the knowledge and skills in the design and development of Web pages. Tutorials in hypertext markup language (HTML) are available on the Web in large numbers, as well as reference and style manuals for the prospective Web page developer. The page shown in Figure 4.25 offers an excellent online tutorial developed at Maricopa University. *HTML is the most commonly used language for creating Web pages, and is not difficult to learn.*

Fig. 4.25 An online tutorial for creating Web pages

http://www.luminet.net/~jackp/success.htm#fig4-25

The Online Career Center (OCC) Homepage

Employment resources exist in abundance on the Internet. At the *Online Career Center* Web site (Figure 4.26), users can easily search for jobs which have been posted on the OCC's electronic job bulletin boards. You can quickly locate employment listings in a particular career category or geographic area by selecting the Search menu at this site. (Also, note that employers can search the résumés posted by interested job seekers from a different menu option.) The OCC includes menu selections for career assistance information, employment events, and a FAQ for using the resources at this online employment center.

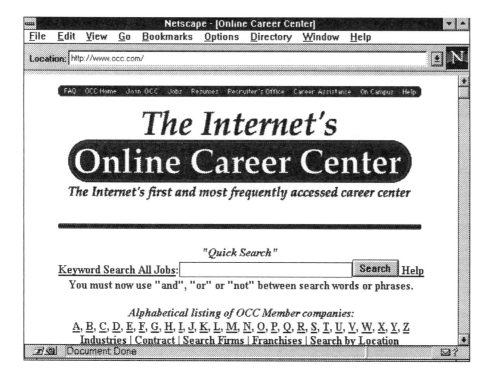

Fig. 4.26 An online career center at a gopher site

http://www.luminet.net/~jackp/success.htm#fig4-26

Searching for Jobs at the OCC Gopher

After selecting the Search option from the *Online Career Center* main menu, I reached the "search screen" (Figure 4.27). Here, I was able to search for employment opportunities by geographic location as well as by company name. Menu options lead the user to keyword searching engines for finding regular and contract employment positions. By following the appropriate menus and carefully reading the on-screen instructions, it is a simple matter to follow these online menus in the job-searching process. Note that hundreds of excellent resources for seeking employment are available on the World Wide Web in addition to the OCC.

Fig. 4.27 Employment seeking at the OCC gopher site

http://www.luminet.net/~jackp/success.htm#fig4-27

Using Online Résumé Banks to Find Employment

One of the popular features of the Internet for job seekers is the availability of a large number of *résumé banks*. Résumé banks allow students to place their "electronic résumés" online for viewing by prospective employers. Currently, the OCC Web site allows users to place one copy of their résumé online at no charge. Figure 4.28 highlights some instructions for submitting online résumés to the OCC site. Note that if your résumé is currently stored in a "word processor" file format, it must first be converted into a standard ASCII text file before e-mailing to OCC.

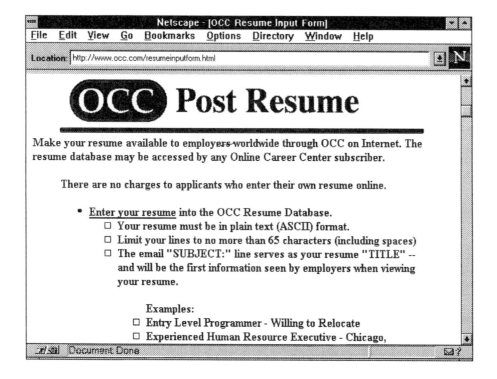

Fig. 4.28 Directions for posting your résumé on the Internet

http://www.luminet.net/~jackp/success.htm#fig4-28

Review Questions

1. Describe your definition of hypertext, and compare it with the typical presentation of text (such as in this printed textbook).

2. Explain what happens when you select or click on a hyperlink on a Web page.

3. What is the difference between a text-only Web browser (such as Lynx) and a graphic-based browser?

4. Name two individuals who contributed to the development of the World Wide Web and their accomplishments.

5. Why do browsers include a back-up option?

6. Describe the purpose of setting bookmarks at sites of interest you may find while browsing the Web.

7. Why were Web search engines developed?

8. Outline the process for using a typical search engine on the Internet.

9. Compare the usage of a search engine with a comprehensive index on the Web (such as *Yahoo*™).

10. Where is the URL address of the current Web page being viewed located on most browsers?

11. If graphics are slowing the loading of Web pages on your browser, what can usually be done to speed things along?

12. When searching for scholarship or fellowship information on the Internet, what should the student be careful to observe regarding the information presented?

13. Describe how a clickable map or graphic picture on a Web page operates.

14. Describe three advantages of e-zines on the Internet relative to printed magazines available on the newsstand.

Exercises

1. Using a search engine, index, or virtual library, locate at least three Web pages with newspapers displayed online and bookmark them.

2. Using a search engine, index, or virtual library, locate at least three e-zines in your area of interest or study and bookmark them.

3. Locate five Web pages which allow students to place their résumés online for viewing by prospective employers and bookmark them.

4. Find the Web homepage of your own college or educational institution. Outline the features and resources available at this page.

5. Locate at least three sites on the Web which will allow you to search for e-mail addresses on the Internet and bookmark them.

6. Find a tutorial on developing Web pages with HTML different from the one presented in the text.

Chapter 5

Newsgroups: Information Sharing Worldwide

5.1 Overview

Newsgroups are the bulletin boards of the Internet. Students who have access to a news server computer (along with their Internet account privileges) can access sometimes many thousands of newsgroups in a variety of general categories. The latest research developments, "issues of the day," and a variety of relevant discussions are often held in the newsgroups. Experts in a variety of fields are frequent contributors to newsgroups which focus on topics relevant to their area of expertise. This text will focus on newsgroups on the Usenet network, which is accessed through the Internet.

A "news reader" program needs to be installed on the local computer system in order to access and contribute to the newsgroups. Newsgroup article "headers" include "subject lines" which describe the nature of individual messages posted to the group. After reading a message posted to a newsgroup, the user can save or print the message as well as post a response to it. Discussion "threads" often develop in newsgroups as the users exchange comments and ideas regarding aspects of a topic under discussion. Frequently Asked Questions (FAQ) lists are an invaluable resource for students learning the use of many Internet tools and resources, including specific details on the Usenet newsgroups. FAQs are freely available to students from various FTP, gopher, and Web sites on the Internet.

5.2 What Are Newsgroups?

Imagine, for just a moment, a dedicated, global computer network called *Usenet* (which can be accessed through the Internet), an exceptionally large "*virtual university*" which allows millions of people to freely enter to explore its resources. In this virtual university are many floors, each of which contains hundreds or even thousands of classrooms (remember this is a "virtual," not a real, university). Further assume that each of these many classrooms on the various floors contains a huge bulletin board spanning the length of each room.

Students who enter one of the classrooms at any time can freely post messages of practically any type on the bulletin board such as notes, articles, abstracts, opinions, stories, thoughts, musings, rantings, ravings, poems, pictures, compositions, critiques, complaints, notices, referrals, suggestions, and warnings.

At any time of the day or night, many hundreds, thousands, or even tens of thousands of individuals can be found milling about in the various classrooms reading or posting responses to the articles and messages on the bulletin boards.

Assume that each classroom has a name on the door corresponding to a specific topic of interest or study. For example, while meandering through the classrooms on the floor of the library named **sci.**, you may notice a room down the hall with the name **sci.archaeology**. Out of curiosity, you take a walk into that room, and after scanning the articles posted on the bulletin board, you realize that they all relate somehow to the science of archaeology.

After milling about various other rooms on the **sci.** floor, and watching in the background as the articles are posted on the boards, you soon arrive at the realization that you must be on the "science floor" of this university, as the bulletin boards in the rooms on that floor all contain articles related to science.

While *lurking* in the background in some of the rooms you enter, you observe that many individuals are posting reply messages to some of the articles posted on the boards, while other people are placing reply messages to previously posted replies! As you look at these giant bulletin boards, the whole arrangement of article messages, replies, and replies to the replies looks rather complex and confusing. However, you soon realize that replies to articles or messages are always placed in a column (usually indented) below the postings they are responding to.

A large group of other people in the room are doing the same as you: standing in the background, and reading all or some of the messages posted by other individuals who previously placed them on the bulletin board. Although these "lurkers" are not necessarily adding their own comments or information to the boards, they are reading the postings which interest them, including the original articles, as well as the replies and "counterreplies." By perusing articles and messages placed on the board and following the discussions in progress, they are keeping abreast of the latest news and information being shared regarding the topics discussed in that classroom.

The virtual university described here is analogous to the operation of the newsgroups (or electronic bulletin boards) which exist on the Usenet computer network, and which can be accessed directly by students through the Internet. There is a voluminous number of newsgroups (more than 40,000 individual Usenet bulletin boards exist at the time of this text's publication), each corresponding to a classroom in an electronic, world-encompassing virtual university.

Newsgroups allow individuals who have a mutual interest in a topic to carry on discussions and share information with each other in a convenient forum, regardless of their geographic location. As discussed in Chapter 2, these groups are similar to the listserv-based discussion lists, accessible through the Internet. Some differences, however, between newsgroups and mailing lists are worthy of mentioning, including the following:

1. Discussion lists use e-mail as the medium for sharing information between members of the group, whereas newsgroups are usually accessed by a connection between the local computer system and a dedicated news server computer on the Internet (which receives regular "newsfeeds" from the Usenet network).

2. Lists are managed by listserv computer servers, which distribute all messages sent by group members to everyone on the mailing list. Newsgroup subscribers can access the article headlines efficiently from the news server and have the option to bypass articles not relevant to their interests.

3. Subscribing and participating in a discussion list requires only a simple e-mailing program (which most students who access the Internet have at their disposal), whereas reading messages placed on the newsgroups requires a *news reader* program as well.

4. Lists require a student to have only an Internet account and e-mail privileges, whereas accessing newsgroups requires the campus computer system to have "access rights" to a news server on the Internet which receives newsfeeds from the Usenet network.

5. Messages placed on newsgroup bulletin boards are typically listed by the various article and response headlines, allowing users to choose which postings they will read in detail. The entire text of messages shared in discussion lists is sent to all members of the group, which can result in large quantities of e-mail messages received by each list member on a daily basis. Often a significant amount of this mail is not of direct relevance to the student's needs or interests, and must be discarded.

Students who are comfortable with their news reader program, and use it frequently to access the latest information being shared on newsgroups of interest, can gain tremendous educational benefits. In research-related groups, for example, the most recent developments are often discussed by experts in many fields of study. By "eavesdropping" on the information and discussions shared on the bulletin boards, students can have exposure to up-to-date reports of progress in their fields of study and gain an invaluable perspective on many subjects by reading the opinions of individuals throughout the world who share information in these virtual classrooms via the Internet.

Unlike the "one-way" knowledge disseminated by a textbook, newsgroups are interactive. Students may read information on an electronic bulletin board and pose a question to the group to clarify an issue, or state their own opinions regarding a topic of interest or discussion. In a sense, the newsgroups can perform the functions of an online classroom, where topics of study are presented, analyzed, discussed, and debated among interested individuals. Unlike an actual classroom in a physical building, however, these virtual classrooms can be frequented by anyone in the world who has access to the Internet newsgroups.

5.3   Steps to Accessing Newsgroups

The steps required for accessing, reading, and contributing to the newsgroups will usually include the following:

1. Logging on to the Internet.

2. Starting a news reader computer program—assuming your campus system has access to a news server computer. (A news reader is software which is required on the local system to access articles and messages from the newsgroups.) Modern Web browsing software programs have the capability of allowing users to read the postings in the various newsgroups.

3. Choosing a newsgroup of interest by browsing a list of those available in various categories, or by selecting a specific one using a search engine.

4. Scanning a list of article and response headlines for recent postings to the newsgroup of interest.

5. Selecting an article or reply message of interest, which will be displayed for viewing in its entirety on the screen.

6. Printing or saving a copy of the article text, if desired.

7. Posting an article or response message to the newsgroup, if the user is allowed privileges to do so and is using a capable news reader program. By choosing New Article (or a similarly named option) from the news reader program menu, an on-screen text editor will appear, allowing the user to type comments into the message form on the screen. When completed, the message can then be directly posted to the newsgroup by selecting the appropriate option from the program's menu.

5.4   Example: Accessing a Music-Related Newsgroup

Using my World Wide Web browser program as a newsgroup "reader," I decided to check the classical guitar newsgroup to see what the latest discussions and "hot topics" are in this area. The listing shown was a display of the most recent articles in this newsgroup, and this list is constantly being updated as users submit new messages to this bulletin board. Only a list of the headlines is shown when browsing a bulletin board. A headline of an article or posting is all that is seen unless the user specifically selects an article or response for viewing in detail. (The title of the posting is often displayed in bold face, followed by the author's name and the total number of lines of text in the article in parentheses.)

Various mail reading programs will display the list of headlines in differing ways. Some allow the user to sort the entries shown by date, author, or subject. Usually, the most recent postings to the newsgroup are shown initially, although the user may also access older articles through menu options in the program. Very old messages posted to bulletin boards are periodically removed and stored in *archive files*, to save space for the constant influx of newer articles and reply postings which continuously stream in. (It is possible to search for information from the newsgroup archives using programs designed for this purpose. The World Wide Web, for example, allows easy access to search engines for exploring information stored in the Usenet archives. Chapter 4 presents an example of the use of a Web search engine designated for this purpose.)

When a conversation in a newsgroup focuses on a subtopic, where users are posting responses to previous responses, the ensuing dialogue is termed a "thread." *Threads* are very common in newsgroups: one individual may post an article pertaining to a specific subject; other users respond to that article, and the original article author (or other readers) responds to the previous responses, initiating a chain of counterresponses which may continue indefinitely as more readers add their "two cents worth" to the discussion. Sometimes conversation threads continue for weeks on end as various users argue (sometimes quite heatedly) or otherwise express their opinions about a discussion topic.

Newsgroup reader programs make it easy for an individual lurking in a newsgroup to follow a threaded discussion, as responses to previous responses are often displayed next to each other for easy reading. On some news readers, a button or menu option is available to follow the thread of the current article or response — automatically opening the next message in the thread for reading.

Newsgroup Header Information

1. The subject title of the article or response. This is a brief description of the nature of the article or posting.

2. The date and time the message was posted to the newsgroup.

3. The return e-mail address of the individual posting the article or response. (Sometimes these addresses are omitted, or are bogus.)

4. The organization with which the individual posting the article is affiliated.

5. The name of the newsgroup (for example, rec.music.classical.guitar).

After reading an article posted about a particular classical guitarist, I decided to post a responding message to the newsgroup. Since I was using a Web browser for reading the news on this bulletin board, it was a simple task for me to send a response. When reading newsgroup articles, a menu button on the browse screen is available to "respond immediately" to the article currently being displayed on the monitor.

After selecting this option, a text editor entry screen (similar to an e-mail message form) appears on the display. The header subject line and my return e-mail address are automatically filled in by the program, so I need only to type the text of my message into the entry form on the screen and click the Send button, and my responding message will be sent to the newsgroup for posting. After some time has elapsed, my message will be available for viewing by thousands of classical guitar aficionados throughout the world via the Internet and this Usenet newsgroup (see Figure 5.1).

Note that news reader programs do not all work in the same fashion, and may use different keys, menu selections, or on-screen buttons to accomplish the

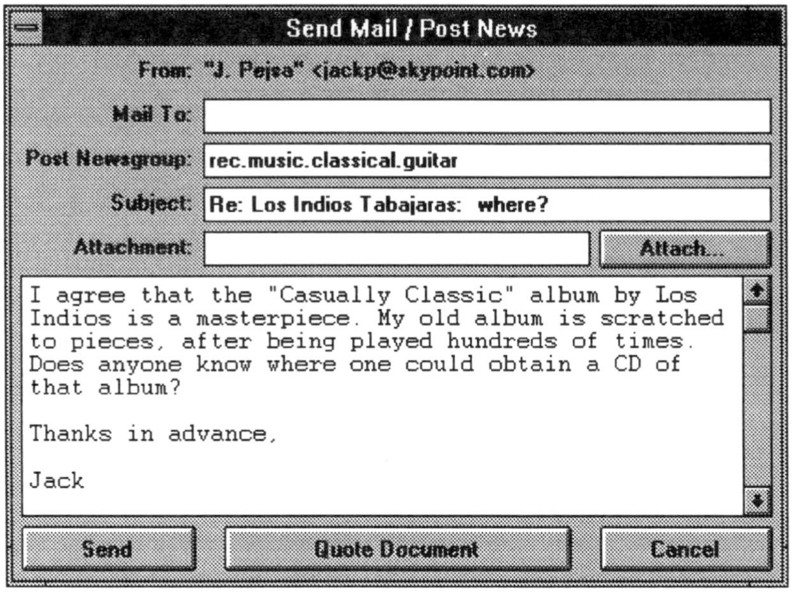

```
┌─────────────────────────────────────────────────────────┐
│  ─           Send Mail / Post News                       │
├─────────────────────────────────────────────────────────┤
│        From: "J. Pejsa" <jackp@skypoint.com>             │
│     Mail To: [                                        ]   │
│ Post Newsgroup: [rec.music.classical.guitar           ]   │
│      Subject: [Re: Los Indios Tabajaras:  where?      ]   │
│   Attachment: [                          ]  [ Attach... ] │
│  ┌──────────────────────────────────────────────────┐▲  │
│  │ I agree that the "Casually Classic" album by Los │   │
│  │ Indios is a masterpiece. My old album is scratched│   │
│  │ to pieces, after being played hundreds of times. │   │
│  │ Does anyone know where one could obtain a CD of  │   │
│  │ that album?                                       │   │
│  │                                                   │   │
│  │ Thanks in advance,                                │   │
│  │                                                   │   │
│  │ Jack                                              │   │
│  └──────────────────────────────────────────────────┘▼  │
│   [    Send    ]   [  Quote Document  ]   [   Cancel   ]  │
└─────────────────────────────────────────────────────────┘
```

Fig. 5.1 A responding message posted to the classical guitar newsgroup

various user functions. Furthermore, although modern Web browsers allow access to the Usenet newsgroups, dedicated news reader client programs often offer many more features which add to the convenience of reading and contributing news articles and response messages to these online bulletin boards.

It may take a few minutes (or several hours) before a message is actually posted to the newsgroup after sending, at which point other individuals may read and respond to it. Newsgroup readers frequently mail private replies directly to another person via standard e-mail (instead of the newsgroup) if the message is personal or not intended for reading by the whole group.

Remember: If your message is meant for only one or two individuals, use e-mail, *not* the newsgroups or discussion lists.

Also, many newsgroups are "moderated," which means that a real human being reads every message before it is accepted for posting to the group. *Moderated newsgroups* are supposed to help eliminate the posting of messages which have no relevance to the newsgroup topic area, or could be construed as offensive to the newsgroup readership. Unmoderated newsgroups are far more common on Usenet, and the messages submitted to these groups are not screened before posting. Consequently, it is unfortunate that on many newsgroups one must wade through a large number of article headers which are not relevant to the subjects under discussion and serve only as an annoyance to readers.

Probably the most severely annoying messages posted to the newsgroups are the spamming articles. These postings are usually a self-serving attempt by very inconsiderate individuals to advertise a product, service, or opinion to a newsgroup's readers, who find such submissions to their group extremely offensive. "Get rich quick" postings (such as MLM, multilevel marketing, rip-offs and "earn $$$ working at home" schemes) are a ubiquitous example of spams commonly seen in the newsgroups. Spamming can usually be recognized by the article headline, which is quite often completely unrelated to the subjects being discussed within the group. Also, *spammers* tend to cross-post to several newsgroups at once, thereby successfully annoying even larger groups of people in the process.

Users who clutter up the Usenet bulletin boards with spams are universally ignored, reproached, or even despised by the online community, and many Internet service providers will immediately withdraw usage privileges from individuals guilty of such activities. Sometimes an entire organization is denied access to Usenet because of the spamming activities of a single individual using the network! It is possible to promote products or services through the Internet, *but not by spamming*.

5.5 General Newsgroup Categories

In the analogy presented earlier, the Usenet newsgroups were presented as a global-reaching virtual university, where each floor corresponded to one general subject. All classrooms on any floor contained bulletin boards with messages related to that subject. For example, on the sci. floor, all the rooms on that floor had bulletin boards related in some way to science.

Let's now expand this analogy a bit by assuming this virtual university consists of a number of independent "virtual buildings," each of which is dedicated to a general type of information studied. As before, the subjects discussed in each building are separated by floor, while subtopics (and sub-subtopics) are explored in the various classrooms through messages posted on bulletin boards.

Each virtual building in the analogy represents how the Usenet newsgroups are separated by general newsgroup categories, which are further separated into individual topics (floors) and subtopics (classrooms). The general categories of newsgroups available on the Internet include the following:

1. **alt.** — alternative newsgroups (whose names begin with **alt.**) consist of a very large number of subject categories in a wide variety of topics, including many which are unusual in content, and some outright bizarre. Controversial, eclectic, and "off-the-mainstream" topics are often included in this category. These groups usually are unmoderated and can vary greatly in their quality of content and usefulness for students.

   A sampling of topics from the top of the list of the thousands of newsgroups in this category includes: adoption, agriculture, alien visitors, amateur computing, "angst," Appalachia, aquaria, archery, architecture, art, Asian movies, astrology, atheism, antique autos, and backrubs.

   Don't forget: academic freedom, Alaskan culture, Batman, binaries (pictures), books and book reviews, boomerangs, breakfast cereal, British comedy, business, cable TV, child support, Chinese text, cooperatives, collecting autographs, college food, comics, consciousness, conspiracy, cyberpunk, dad's rights, Desert Storm, dreams, disabled education, exotic music, fans of Jimmy Buffett, feminism, and fishing.

   And of course there are: college folklore, forgery, fractals, games, guitar, hackers, horror, hot rods, humor, individualism, journalism, magic, meditation, missing children, music, mythology, paranormal, personal ads, politics, privacy, prose, psychology, punk, quotations, rap, recovery, religion, rock and roll, romance, satellite TV, self-improvement, skateboarding, snowmobiles, sports, support groups, surfing, toys, TV, war, wolves, and many hundreds more.

2. **k12.** — this category consists of newsgroups for students of elementary through secondary ages (or their teachers or administrators) to share communications, work together on projects, or discuss ideas in K–12 education. Young people of all ages are frequent contributors to the bulletin boards in the general **k12.** category.

   Included in this general category are the following topical areas: art curricula, business education, teaching computer literacy, health and physical education, home economics, career education, mathematics, science curricula, music and performing arts, social studies, history, language arts, German, Spanish, French, Russian (students may practice with native speakers over these Usenet newsgroups), and a number of "individual project channels" which may be used for a variety of educational purposes.

3. **comp.** — these newsgroups are all related to the topic of computers. Very large numbers of subcategories (and subsubcategories) exist which allow

users to exchange information and ideas regarding hundreds of computer-related subjects.

4. **misc.** — these newsgroups don't fit conveniently into any other subject category so they're placed in the miscellaneous class of groups. A large range and variety of topics is discussed in the hundreds of bulletin boards in this general category.

   Examples of topics covered within the **misc.** category include: activism, technical books, consumer interests, education, entrepreneurs, fitness, articles for sale, computer buying and selling, diabetes, intellectual property rights, investments, real estate, jobs offered (entry, contract, and permanent employment), résumé postings online, children's issues, use of computers by children, legal ethics, news from India, taxes, rural living, items wanted to buy, and writing.

5. **news.** — these groups all contain information and resources related to the newsgroups on the Internet. For example, novice users can obtain a wealth of information regarding the use of the bulletin boards by reading and asking questions in the **news.newusers.questions** group.

   It is highly recommended that new users of the newsgroups visit the **news.newusers.questions** group as contributors may participate in discussions, ask questions, and learn from others regarding the use of this valuable Internet tool.

   Novices ("newbies") who post messages or questions to this group can learn from experienced users how to perform various tasks related to the newsgroups, including how to subscribe to groups and post messages, where to find the names and topics covered by new groups being formed, how to locate the frequently asked questions list for a particular newsgroup (the FAQ is a list of typically asked questions and answers for users who are newcomers to a newsgroup), and any other questions or problems they may be having in using the Internet bulletin boards.

   Subtopics in the **news.** bulletin boards include: Usenet policies, news administration, technical aspects of network news, conference announcements, new user information and questions, future newsgroup technologies, lists of newsgroups, maps of Usenet and traffic flow, and news reading software.

6. **sci.** — these newsgroups all relate in some way to science. A tremendous range and variety of scientific disciplines are represented in this general category.

(Any student who is engaged in research in a scientific topic, or is writing a paper or project relating to modern advances in science, should certainly peruse the available sci. newsgroups for those that are appropriate to the area of study. Many "world experts" closely monitor, and frequently contribute to, newsgroups in their area of specialty.)

A sampling of the topics covered in the sci. category includes: aeronautics, anthropology, archaeology, astronomy, Hubble telescope, biology, ecology, chemistry, classics, cognitive science, cryonics, cryptology, economic research, science of education, energy, engineering (biomedical, chemical, civil, manufacturing, mechanical, environmental), fractals, geophysical fluid dynamics, geology, meteorology, image processing, linguistics, "life extension," logic, materials, math, medicine, optics, philosophy, physics, polymers, psychology, research methods, space, statistics, systems, and "virtual worlds."

7. soc. — these groups are associated with society, social structures, and different cultures of the world. Since the Internet and Usenet are worldwide in scope and coverage, contributors from a large number of countries located throughout the world are represented in this category.

A sampling of some soc. newsgroup topical areas includes: college and campus life, graduate education, couples, feminism, history, libraries, men's issues, pen pals, politics, religion, roots, singles, veterans, and women's issues. Cultures included are Afghanistani, African, African-American, Arabic, Argentinian, Asian-American, Austrian, Baltic, Bangladeshi, Bosnian-Herzegovina, Brazilian, British, Bulgarian, Canadian, Croatian, Chinese, European, Filipino, French, German, Indian, Indonesian, Iranian, Italian, Japanese, Korean, Lebanese, Mexican, Nepali, Netherlandic, Nordic, Pakistani, Peruvian, Polish, Portuguese, Romanian, Singaporean, Soviet, Spanish, Taiwanese, Tamili, Thai, Turkish, Ukrainian, Venezuelan, Vietnamese, and Yugoslavian.

8. bit. — these groups (whose names begin with bit.) are newsfeeds from a separate computer network with the name *Bitnet*. Many e-mail-based discussion lists administered by listserv computers (as detailed in Chapter 2) are accessible through this newsgroup category.

A sampling of the newsgroups in this category includes: autism, blindness, computers and health, technology transfer, disarmament, educational technology, electronic music, ethics, ethology, filmmaking, fractals, games, history, law schools, libraries, medical student forum, medical libraries, K–12 physics, politics, postcard collecting, graduate psychology, romance readers, supercomputers, scuba diving, secondary math education, travel, electronic publishing, and word processing.

9. clari. — these newsgroups (whose names all begin with clari.) are news-feeds from a commercial news-gathering network called *clarinet*. There is a separate and additional cost for an organization wishing to retrieve *clari-net* newsfeeds, so not all schools may have access to the newsgroups in this category.

A small sampling of the clari. groups includes newsfeeds in the following areas: business news and headlines, Associated Press newsbriefs, enter-tainment news, movies, music, Chicago Board of Trade, daily gold and dollar prices, general economy reports, news reviews, stock market analyses, Dow Jones averages, the current day in history, television, weather reports, major storm forecasts, business and economic newsbriefs, finance and currency, and news by various industries (aviation, banking, broadcasting, construction, food, health, insurance, manufacturing, min-ing, and retail sales).

10. rec. — these newsgroups include discussions, information, and resources related to recreation, sports, games, many hobbies, and leisure activities of all types. It is quite probable that your favorite sport or pastime is repre-sented by some newsgroup of avid participants in the rec. general cate-gory. To illustrate a rather pathetic example: a student from Minnesota, on some typical -42° F day in January, could check on the current weather and windsurfing conditions in Maui (for what masochistic purpose, I can't guess) by checking the rec.windsurfing newsgroup.

The rec. newsgroups include the following small set of sample areas of interest: antiques, aquaria, animation, body art, bonsai, books, cinema, comics, dance, interactive fiction, drum corps, marching, arts, movies, po-ems, prose, art marketplace, science fiction, theater, TV, audio, autos, aviation, "back country," bicycles, birds, boats, climbing, collecting, crafts, equestrian, folk dancing, food, board games, backgammon, bridge, chess, gardening, guns, humor, hunting, kites, martial arts, model rail-roading, motorcycles, music, Mensa, outdoor activities, parks, pets, photog-raphy, puzzles, amateur radio, roller coasters, running, scuba diving, sports (baseball, basketball, cricket, fencing, football, golf, hockey, Olympics, wrestling, rowing, rugby, soccer, swimming, table tennis, triathlon, volley-ball, water skiing), travel, video, windsurfing, and woodworking.

11. **talk.** — these newsgroups often are related to "topics of the day," including a wide range of politically oriented discussions. The dialogues in these groups can get quite heated at times, as controversial subjects are commonly debated by the participants.

A brief sampling of topics under discussion in a recent visit by the author to the **talk.** newsgroups included: abortion, environmental concerns, evolution vs. creationism debates, philosophy, politics (animals, China, cryptology, drugs, guns, medicine, Mideast, space, theory), rape, religion, and "rumors."

5.6   News Reading Software

It is not difficult to gain access to the Usenet newsgroups (and others) on the Internet. As discussed in Section 5.3, your Internet account must be allowed privileges to connect with a news server computer and have access rights to it.

If your computer (or the network to which it is connected) has access privileges to a news server, this means that you have the capability of reading and posting messages on the Usenet bulletin boards through this server.

(If you configure your own news reader program, you will need to enter the name of the news server computer you are accessing. Sometimes you will also need to enter a user name and password necessary for personal access to a particular news server. Ask your lab attendant or computer systems administrator for specific information regarding the name, access rights, and the number and variety of newsgroup categories carried by the server used through your campus network.)

Assuming you have access rights to a news server which gets newsfeeds from Usenet, including a large number of newsgroups, you will need to use one software tool to read the messages posted on these boards (and to post messages of your own, if desired).

The tool needed to access the newsgroups is called a news reader program. A news reader is software which is installed on your local computer (or on the network to which your computer is connected) which allows you to subscribe to newsgroups, read messages and threads of discussions within groups, and contribute reply or "new message" postings of your own.

If you are connected to a large campus computer network, there may likely be a news reader program installed on the system. Ask your computer system administrator or lab assistant about the appropriate news reading software for students, how to access it, and *where the documentation for the program is located.*

For students who are installing their own news reading software applications, there are many to choose from, all of which work within most of the operating environments of modern personal computer systems. Many news readers are easily available as shareware through FTP sites on the Internet. FTP sites for downloading shareware are discussed in Chapter 6 of this text.

Many commercial packages (including integrated Internet application "software suites") include a news reader as one of the programs in the package. As stated previously, larger computer systems (such as Unix- and Vax-based campus systems) often include news reading software with the standard applications they make available to all eligible users of the system.

In the examples discussed in the text, you may have noticed that a World Wide Web browser was used to access and contribute to the newsgroups being discussed. Modern browsers include this capability, along with its other powerful functions for searching, locating, accessing, and sharing information via the Internet. Newsgroup access is a very useful feature to integrate with a Web browser, since it isn't necessary to install and learn a separate news reader program for accessing Usenet.

It should be noted, however, that "dedicated" news reader programs have additional features that may not be available when you access the newsgroups through a Web browser. If you become a real Usenet aficionado, and spend a large amount of time reading and contributing to the newsgroups, you may wish to try using programs designed specifically for this purpose.

5.7   Frequently Asked Questions (FAQs) Documents

One sign of an experienced Internet user is that person's awareness of the significant value of the frequently asked questions (FAQs) documents for practically any tool or resource used on the Internet, including the Usenet newsgroups.

FAQ compilations exist for, and are filled with valuable information about virtually any Internet-related topic which exists, and for each topic covered there is usually included a large selection of "typical questions" asked by new or inexperienced users (along with the answers to those questions, of course).

Most of the established Usenet newsgroups maintain FAQs for the newbies who are interested in joining and participating in the group. Experienced contributors get weary of repeatedly answering the same questions asked by newcomers when they initially join a group. Rather than continually responding to these often repeated questions, members of the newsgroup usually compile a list of many of the frequently asked questions.

Answers are provided for each of the questions in this document, and the entire file of questions and answers is posted to the newsgroup on a regular basis. Also, this file is placed at various FAQ archive sites on the Internet.

At the time of printing, a large number of newsgroup FAQs were available on the Web at a site maintained by Ohio State University at the URL address: http://www.cis.ohio-state.edu/hypertext/faq/usenet/FAQ-List.html.

Note: URLs (uniform resource locators) *are the addresses of Web pages and are discussed in detail in Chapter 3 of this text.*

In summary, FAQs are question-and-answer compilations which have been prepared, filed, and archived for the benefit of any interested Internet users. Literally tens of thousands of FAQ documents exist for the many thousands of newsgroups, as well as for a significant variety of other topics of interest.

Summary

Newsgroups are a valuable Internet communication and information-sharing resource for students. Newsgroups (frequently called electronic bulletin boards) allow Internet users to freely exchange information, pass messages, and discuss specific topics of interest with other Internet users. These bulletin boards (the majority of which exist on the Usenet network) are separated into logical categories and subcategories. Some of the general categories of newsgroups include alt. (alternative), bit. (Bitserv network groups linked to the listserv discussion lists), clari. (a commercial, fee-based news-providing service network), comp. (computer related), k12. (discussions about and with elementary-age through secondary-age kids), misc. (a little bit of everything), news. (information and discussions related to the newsgroups and Usenet), rec. (recreation, sports, and leisure activities), sci. (science related), soc. (society and cultures), and talk. (politically oriented discussions, debates, and diatribes).

In order to access newsgroups, a student needs permission rights to connect with a news server computer. News servers perform the function of news message "post offices." In addition to access to a news server, the user needs to have a news reader program installed on the local computer, or available for use by students on the campus computer network.

News readers allow the student Internet user to list available newsgroups by name and search for particular newsgroups of interest, subscribe to newsgroups, list the subject headers for a group, open messages of interest, and respond to messages posted (or create new "articles" for posting to the newsgroup).

Large computer systems typically install news reading software for their Internet users, whereas smaller computer systems need additional software packages installed on the system (either on each local machine or on the network file server). News reading software is available from shareware archives at FTP sites on the Internet and is also available commercially. Modern Web browsers perform a respectable job as news readers.

Conversations in a newsgroup can branch "off the track" to separate topics, or narrow the focus of part of the discussion to specific aspects of the main topic. Such detours from the main focus of the original article are termed threads. Controversial articles tend to generate many responses and counterargument threads in a newsgroup.

Since many experts in their field regularly lurk in and contribute to newsgroups in their area of expertise, students are encouraged to periodically read postings in the newsgroups which apply to their academic area of specialty or interest.

Frequently asked questions (FAQ) documents are an exceptionally valuable, and freely available, resource for newsgroup (and all Internet) users. These documents list common questions asked by newcomers (newbies) to a newsgroup, or provide general information about a given topic, resource, tool, or area of knowledge. Many thousands of FAQs are available for the very large number of newsgroups in existence, as well as for a large variety of other Internet-related topics. FAQ documents are posted to newsgroups regularly and are also available at FTP sites, which allow you to easily download these files to your own computer system.

Review Questions

1. What software is needed in order to access newsgroups?

2. What is the purpose and function of a news server?

3. What is meant by "lurking" in a newsgroup?

4. What information is included in a news article header?

5. How do newsgroup discussion threads develop?

6. Explain the advantages and possible disadvantages of moderated newsgroups.

7. List five newsgroup general categories and the types of topics which may be discussed within each category.

8. Which general newsgroup category includes jobs-offered listings?

9. What is the first step to perform if you are not sure how to use a particular software application (such as a news reader)?

10. What is the name given to a newcomer to a Usenet newsgroup?

11. What is the most efficient way for a newsgroup newcomer to learn the appropriate discussion topics in a newsgroup?

12. What type of Internet sites offer shareware on the Internet for downloading by interested users?

13. Explain what a registered copy of a shareware program is.

14. Name two advantages of the use of a Web browser as a news reader.

15. Why are FAQ documents prepared for many newsgroups?

16. How can FAQs be downloaded from sites on the Internet?

Exercises

1. Assuming you have access to a news server computer, join the group **news.newusers.questions** and describe the questions (and their answers) that are posted to that group.

2. Join one group in the following general newsgroup categories, and describe the nature of the conversations in each group:

   alt.

   sci.

   rec.

   news.

   soc.

   comp.

3. List five newsgroups, in any general categories, which may directly apply to the courses of study in your major. Explain how these newsgroups could be used effectively in your academic areas of interest.

4. Write a one-page "crib sheet" on the use of your news reader program. Outline each function of the program and how to access it. Describe how to locate the documentation for the program.

Chapter 6

Resource Site Types on the Internet

6.1   Overview

In addition to the World Wide Web network of hypertext-based pages accessible online, other powerful tools have been developed during the evolution of the Internet for accessing valuable Internet resources:

Telnet allows the student to access other computer systems at distant colleges and universities, as well as research, commercial, and government facilities. A telnet client software package needs to be running locally to log on to the remote telnet server computer.

FTP is a facility for transferring files reliably between computers over the Internet. Many archives of useful information, resources, software, data, and multimedia documents exist freely for downloading by interested Internet users at anonymous FTP sites. A searching tool, Archie, is available for locating FTP sites of interest on the Internet.

Gopher servers on the Internet present a menu interface to users for easily accessing a variety of resource types. Many college campus computer systems allow access by the public to sections of their resource libraries and other online facilities through gopher sites. Veronica is a software tool accessible at many gopher sites which searches the Internet for gopher server menus related to topics of interest.

WAIS tools allow users on the Internet to search databases stored on remote computer systems. Entering keywords into the search engine makes the process of finding data in remote archives a simple task.

6.2   Telnet Access Sites

One of the most prominent advantages of the Internet is that it allows the *sharing of resources* between members of the world community. Many libraries, educational institutions, and research and government facilities allow public access to their computer systems.

A telnet site on the Internet is a computer system running special software (a telnet server program) which allows access by remote users who have permission to use the system's resources. A public telnet server installed on a site (such as a campus system) allows anyone to access that computer server provided that person is connected to the Internet and is running a telnet client program on the local computer system. (Telnet sites were introduced in Section 3.3.)

One advantage of using telnet is that it allows users the capability of accessing computer programs available on "someone else's" computer when those facilities aren't available on the local system. For example, a Campus Wide Information System (CWIS) is an electronic information repository available on a computer server which allows people (who may be geographically distant) to access a large number of campus information resources through the Internet.

Some other types of software packages (programs) that can be accessed on remotely located computers (using telnet software) are the client programs for accessing the various Internet resources such as FTP, gopher, WWW, Archie, WAIS, and IRC. For example, if a student's local computer system does not have a WAIS server (for searching databases on the Internet), it is possible to use WAIS facilities remotely by telnetting to a different system (through the Internet), logging on, and accessing the WAIS services at the remote system using this tool.

Campus Library Systems Worldwide Are Accessed by Telnet

Many libraries allow telnet access through the Internet listing their holdings, and invite visitors to search their library catalogues. Telnet servers on the Internet which allow access by the general public (without an account on the local system) are referred to as public telnet sites. Students who gain facility with telnet have the opportunity to use the libraries and research materials of the best educational and research organizations in all parts of the world! In Figure 6.1, academic works related to the composer Beethoven are researched via telnet.

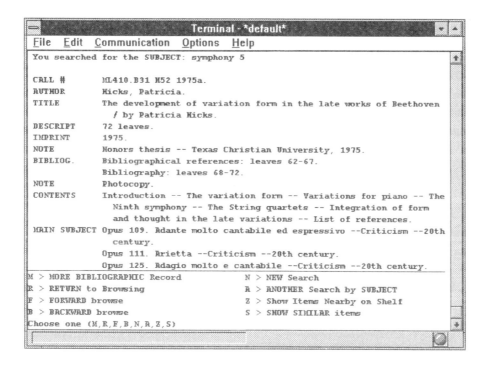

**Fig. 6.1 Researching Beethoven at San Jose
State University through telnet**

Steps to Using Telnet for Accessing Remote Computers

It isn't difficult to log on to other computer systems over the Internet and access electronic-based resources remotely which are not available on your local system. If you are using a modern "windowed" telnet client program installed on your computer or network, review the documentation or Help system for information on connecting to remote telnet servers. If you're using a text-based system (such as an older Unix, Vax, or DOS-based "command-driven" operating system), you will need to do the following:

1. Log on to the Internet.

2. Assuming you have a telnet client program installed on your local computer or network, start the program (ask your instructor or lab assistant to assist you in the use of this tool, if necessary).

An alternative way to access a telnet site on the Internet is through your Web browser—assuming you have a telnet client program installed on your system.

If you click your mouse on a hot link on the screen which your browser recognizes as a telnet site, it will start the telnet client program installed on your system and attempt to connect to the site you have selected.

If you are not accessing telnet through the Web or gopher, the command to start your telnet client program on older systems is **telnet** (followed by the name of the site). To connect by telnet to the *Harvard Online Library Information System* (*Hollis*), for example, I would enter the command:

telnet hollis.harvard.edu

Always check the Help system or written documentation on the commands necessary for using any software application tools, including the client programs used to access Internet resource types discussed.

3. Enter the name of the telnet site, or its IP address. (IP addresses and site names are discussed in Section 3.5.) Connect to the site.

    Alternatively, after starting the telnet client, you may attempt to connect with a server by using the Open command. For example, (after starting my telnet client program), typing the following command will attempt to connect my local computer with the public library system at Harvard:

open hollis.harvard.edu

4. Assuming you successfully connect to a telnet server, you will usually be asked to enter a log-in name (and sometimes a password) in order to gain entry. Sometimes the remote computer will ask for your terminal type as well.

    If you are asked to enter your terminal type, selecting the VT-100 option is often a safe choice. This makes your local computer behave like an older VT-100 text-based terminal. Moving the cursor around the screen on a remote telnet computer (as well as various other text-editing operations) may often be significantly different from the methods you regularly use on your local computer system. Luckily, most telnet systems provide on-screen instructions for assisting users in navigating the menus, or for launching any Internet client programs available for public use.

    (Logging in to telnet servers is discussed in Section 3.3.) At public sites, usually no password is required, and a generic entry (such as **Public**) is frequently used when asked for a log-in name. If you are accessing a telnet server from a Web page (as we will do in the examples beginning on page 124), instructions are usually presented on the page for logging in as a public user at the remote site. Also, sometimes a "port number" must be entered as well, which is usually stated in the instructions presented on the screen.

5. After you're successfully logged in, you may access any publicly available facilities existing at the remote site. Carefully read any instructions presented on the screen for assistance in finding the resources or tools you wish to explore on the remote system. To exit from the remote computer system, use the Close command. Finally, the Quit command will terminate your client program, after you've finished your telnetting activities for the time being.

Using Telnet to Access Harvard's Online Library

Libraries often allow telnet access to some of their resources for public use via the Internet. Figure 6.2 displays the main menu at the *Harvard Online Library Information System (HOLLIS)*. Note the access to card catalogs, a database of information on the reserve list, a guide to Harvard libraries, legal and anthropological indexes, an ERIC educational database search engine, information and journal articles in physics, psychology, and religion, in addition to an "Expanded Academic Index." If you are able to reach the opening menu at *HOLLIS*, entering **ER** (followed by Return) takes you to the ERIC index screen.

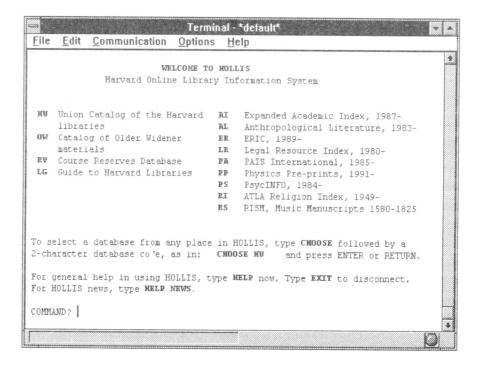

Fig. 6.2 Accessing Harvard's online library through telnet

telnet://hollis.harvard.edu

Accessing the ERIC Research Database via Telnet

ERIC (Educational Resources Information Center) is a large index of journal articles focusing on research in education-related fields. By starting my telnet client program and logging on to the online system at Harvard University, entering **ER** on the main menu transfers me immediately to the ERIC search screen shown in Figure 6.3. A principal advantage of telnet is that it allows users the capability of accessing powerful tools and resources (such as the ERIC index) which may be accessible on another institution's computer system (especially when these resources are not available on the local campus network).

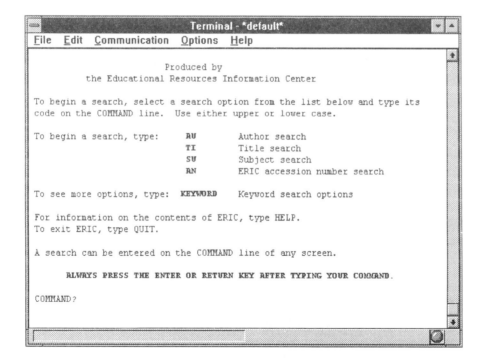

Fig. 6.3 ERIC education resources at Harvard Library

Accessing a University Telnet Site Through a Web Page

The Web page illustrated in Figure 6.4 allows access to the University of Minnesota's public telnet server. As discussed previously, in order to access telnet sites through a Web browser, I must have a telnet client program installed along with my browser program. When I click on admin.ais.umn.edu, my browser will automatically start my telnet client program and attempt to connect me with the Minnesota server. Note that the "launching" Web page pictured here gives me clear instructions for logging in to the server, including details on entering the terminal type (VT-100) that I will use. (As discussed previously, when requested to enter a terminal type, selecting VT-100 is usually a reasonable option.)

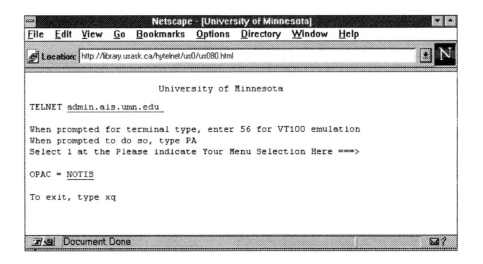

Fig. 6.4 Linking from the Web to a university telnet site

http://www.luminet.net/~jackp/success.htm#fig6-4

http://library.usask.ca/HyTelnet/us0/us080.html

Navigating Menus at the Remote Telnet Site

One point to remember about telnet sites is that you (the user) are truly logged on to "someone else's" computer system. Because computers are not all alike (nor are the programs which run on them), it is not always obvious how to "navigate" around the menus on the remote system. It is important to take your time, and read the screens carefully. In addition, don't forget the Help key, which is available on many telnet systems. At the command prompt, type **help** or **?** for assistance, or choose the appropriate selection from the menu. (Various programs use differing keystrokes, commands, or menu items to access Help—read the screens.) To enter the "Student Access System" at the University of Minnesota site (as shown in Figure 6.5), you must enter **13**.

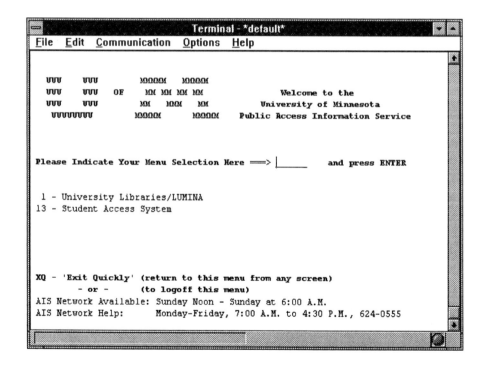

Fig. 6.5 The University of Minnesota libraries telnet site

NASA *Spacelink* Telnet Site: Main Menu

At the time this text was written, NASA's *Spacelink* site was available through public telnet. At this site, it was possible to access educational services and instructional materials created at NASA, the latest space news including Space Shuttle updates and information about projects underway, hot topics at *Spacelink*, and the FAQ on NASA's online resources (Figure 6.6). After connecting to *Spacelink* and viewing the sign-on message, the user entered **guest** when asked for a log-in name. To enter the correct log-in name or password at a public telnet site, remember to read the screens carefully, since that information is often provided for the convenience of guest users of the site.

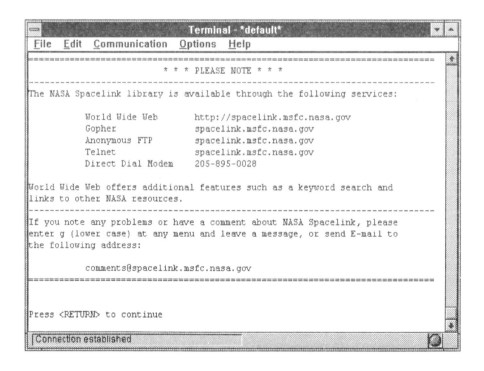

Fig. 6.6 The opening screen at NASA's *Spacelink* old telnet site

Space Shuttle Updates at NASA via Telnet

Recent information relating to the Space Shuttle program is shown in this screen of the NASA *Spacelink* telnet site (Figure 6.7). In many situations, there is simply no better way to find the very latest up-to-date information or late-breaking news on a set of topics or issues than by telnetting straight to the source of information you're seeking.

Logging on to other college computer systems through telnet can provide you with an "inside look" at the events happening at another school, and also may give you access to the electronic library system as well as other campus news and resources. Many information systems (such as libraries) have not installed Web sites to access their resources, and telnet is the only means of connecting to them, so the student researcher is encouraged to gain facility with this tool!

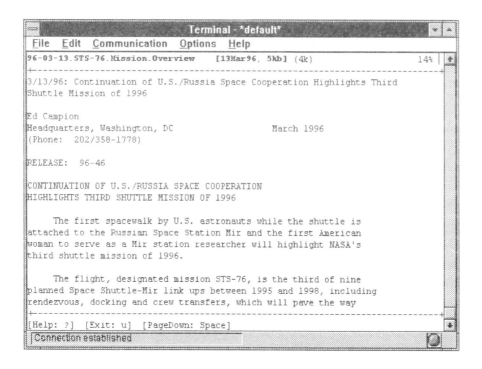

**Fig. 6.7 Reading recent Space Shuttle news
at NASA *Spacelink* via telnet**

Searching Online Libraries Worldwide with *HyTelnet*

Considering that many thousands of computer systems offer public telnet access through the Internet, deciding *which* telnet site to explore is not always an easy task. Luckily, an exceptionally convenient software searching tool called *HyTelnet* has been developed which allows a user to search for appropriate telnet sites by topical category (Figure 6.8). *HyTelnet* indexes are available for many public telnet sites on the Internet. *HyTelnet* is also readily available through many gopher sites as well as on the World Wide Web.

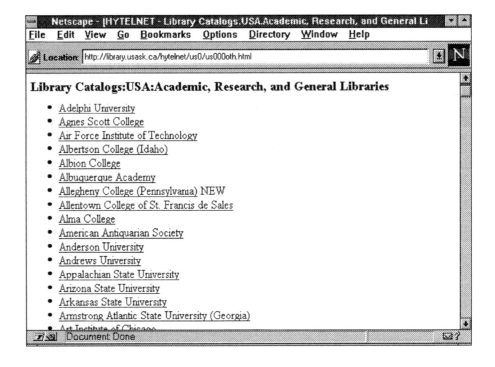

Fig. 6.8 A *HyTelnet* index of online library catalogs available online in the United States

http://www.luminet.net/~jackp/success.htm#fig6-8

Searching Databases at CARL Through Telnet

One of the most powerful features of the Internet is its ability to allow users from all parts of the world to rapidly search literally thousands of databases of information on a nearly infinite range of topics. In Figure 6.9, I telnetted to a site which offers access to portions of the very comprehensive CARL (Colorado Alliance for Research Libraries) research database. Students investigating a subject of interest may wish to use the Uncover option at CARL, which (at the time this text was written) allowed users to look up bibliographic information and research journal publications at no cost.

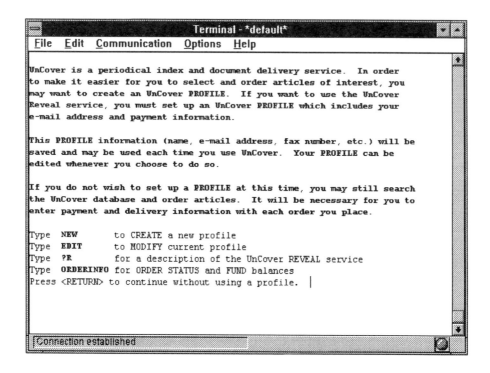

**Fig. 6.9 Using CARL's Uncover option to
search a database for research articles**

Finding Research Articles by Author at CARL

To test CARL in action, I telnetted to **database.carl.org** and chose the Uncover option. (At the time this text was written, using Uncover was free of charge, but note that more powerful features of CARL, including electronic "document delivery," were available for a fee.) After carefully following the directions on the screen, I was easily able to perform an author search on the educational researcher Raymond Kulhavy. Note that the menu of options informing the user which key to press next is near the bottom of the screen. Uncover produced the listing of articles illustrated in Figure 6.10.

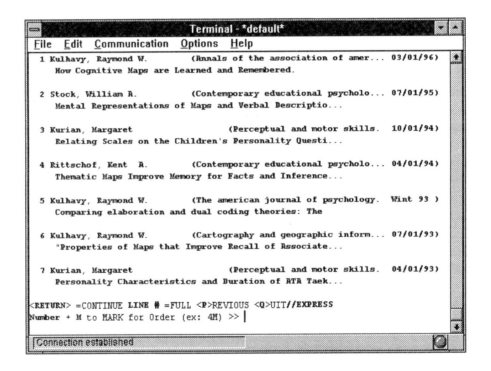

Fig. 6.10 Using CARL's Uncover option to find articles by an educational researcher

6.3   Anonymous FTP Sites

Anonymous FTP sites on the Internet are computers running computer servers which manage a "library" of documents that are available to public users at most any time (and at no cost). Information is stored on these servers to be shared with any interested individuals who access them through the Internet. Files and documents can be downloaded (and sometimes uploaded) by users, as explained in Section 3.3.

For the student Internet user, knowledge of how to access FTP sites on the Internet, retrieve information, and search the many worldwide archives for topics of interest can be a great educational advantage. Many thousands of educational, research, government, nonprofit, and commercial institutions make freely available very large amounts and varieties of information, as well as access to databases, software, graphics, sounds, music, video, and countless other resources through FTP sites.

Downloading a file (such as a document or computer program) from an FTP site refers to the process of transferring a file from a server to a user (client) who requests it.

Most FTP client programs also include the capability of uploading files from the remote site to the FTP server. For example, a student who has written a poem may wish to upload it to an FTP archive on the Internet which allows open access for poetry submissions by users.

Since some files on FTP sites are very large, they can require a considerable amount of time and storage space for the downloading (or uploading) operation. It is often more efficient (and courteous to your fellow Internet users) to download large documents and files when the Internet is less busy, such as late in the evening.

Anonymous FTP Sites: A Library Analogy

Imagine thousands of libraries in different locations throughout the world which allowed anyone to enter at will for browsing a selection of documents, books, images, magazines, journals, audiotapes, or other resource types stored there, and to copy any information found useful (*free of charge*) to take home for storage in personal file cabinets, bookshelves, galleries, or tape libraries.

Suppose, further, that someone could enter any of these libraries (within a few seconds) 24 hours a day, every day of the year! In addition, since anyone would be allowed into these libraries, a library card would not be necessary for entry. Upon signing in, when the librarian asked for visitors' names, they would simply enter **Anonymous** onto the sign-up sheet.

This mythical worldwide distribution of "anonymous entry" libraries, which allow users to browse resources and reproduce materials to take home as they choose, is analogous to the anonymous FTP sites available in large numbers on the Internet. These sites allow users to enter locations in a remote computer's file system, browse the directories for information of interest, and "take home" (download) copies of any files, documents, audiovisual resources, or computer programs they wish to obtain.

When entering a remote computer system's anonymous FTP server via the Internet, it is necessary only to enter **Anonymous** when asked for a user name upon logging in. If the library is not too busy at the time, users are allowed entry and can subsequently browse the resources at this FTP site and download to their own computer systems any materials or files of interest.

Depending on the size of the files being transferred, the type of connection to the Internet in use, and the amount of traffic on the network at the time, the time for downloading files may vary from a few seconds to several minutes (or hours). Speed of data transfer over the Internet is determined by the current "congestion" of electronic traffic it is experiencing as well as the type of connection in use. FTPing directly to a remote server through a modem connected to a telephone line can make downloading files from a server a very slow process.

Steps to Accessing Files at Anonymous FTP Sites

1. Log on to the Internet.

2. If you already know the name or address of the FTP site you wish to visit, proceed to step 4.

3. To look up FTP sites of interest, you can access various search engines such as Archie (which is installed on many systems or is available at shareware archives). You can also search for FTP sites at gopher and Web sites (to be discussed later in this chapter).

4. Start the FTP client program. On text-based systems (such as many older Unix or Vax computers still used on college campuses), you likely will type the **ftp** command to start the program. When using a Web browser or

gopher client program, simply selecting the file of interest will initiate the downloading process.

Commands for performing FTP operations using a "standalone" client program are discussed later in this chapter.

On modern "windowed" user interfaces to computers (such as the typical Macintosh or Windows-based PC), clicking on the FTP icon in a network folder may start the FTP program.

5. Enter the IP address or name of the FTP server onto the entry screen or by typing the **open** command. When asked for a log-in name, enter **anonymous**.

6. Enter your e-mail address when asked for a password. This is a standard practice when logging onto anonymous FTP servers.

7. Browse the directories in the library by using the **cd** command (or by clicking on the file(s) of your choice in a windowed environment).

8. Read the index or readme files to learn more details about the files in the various directories and subdirectories. Simply selecting the files with the mouse will open them for viewing in a windowed program. On "command-based" systems, enter the command **binary** (followed by Enter), and then **get index.txt** (or whatever the name of the documentation file may be in that directory).

9. Download any files desired by using the **get** command, or by selecting them with the mouse. Type **close** to disconnect from the FTP server.

The Basic FTP Commands

If the FTP client program you are using is command based, it requires you to issue program commands by typing them in at the keyboard. After connecting to an FTP server, the following commands are understood by most FTP servers. *Consult the Help system on your FTP client program.*

Command	Description	Example
1. cd	*Change to a different directory*	cd /mirrors
2. dir	*List files in the current directory*	dir
3. dir	more	*List files a screen at a time*	dir	more

4.	get	*Download a file*	get mypoems.zip
5.	put	*Upload a file*	put c:\mypoems.zip
6.	open	*Attempts connecting you to a server*	open ftp.coast.net
7.	close	*Disconnect from a server*	close
8.	quit	*Exit the FTP client program*	quit
9.	lcd	*Change local directory*	lcd c:\internet

10. text   *Puts you in text mode which means you are now capable of downloading ASCII text documents only! Many files at FTP archives are nontext (binary) files. Unless you are sure the files you wish to download are text files, use the binary command, before using the Get command to retrieve the file.*

11. binary   *Prepares you for downloading any type of file. This is the preferred mode in FTP for downloading any type of non-text file.*

BEWARE OF VIRUSES!

In Section 2.12, which discussed sending attached files through e-mail, I issued a warning to remain extremely cautious about accepting attached documents to your system from unknown sources. Virus-infected programs and documents which are shared through the Internet can pose an imminent (and sometimes catastrophic) failure to your computer or network! The same risks to damage inflicted upon your system by infected files received via e-mail are posed by downloading documents from any unknown sources using FTP. Many FTP and e-mail client programs will *automatically* execute infected programs without the user's ability to halt the process and damage incurred! The potential devastating effects of viruses cannot be overstated.

Never run a program, open a document, or start any application which you have received through FTP or e-mail file attachment unless you are *sure* that the information is being obtained from a reputable source. *When in doubt—don't!* Consult your instructor, system administrator, or lab attendant first, if necessary. Also, the latest "virus-checking" software should be installed on all Internet-connected computers.

Types of Information Available by FTP

A tremendous amount of useful information is freely available for downloading at thousands of FTP sites distributed throughout the world to anyone with Internet access who has the appropriate FTP client software installed on a local computer system.

An FTP client program allows your local computer or network to establish a connection and carry on an electronic conversation with an FTP server computer located somewhere on the worldwide Internet.

Resource types available through FTP sites on the Internet include the following examples:

- *Documentation* of software of all types, including Internet tools (such as FTP client programs, news readers, mailing programs, and telnet applications).

- *Graphics* files, including digitized photographs, clip art (many of which you may download and use in your own documents), drawings, maps, and illustrations.

- *Information and resources* on computer programming languages of many types and functions.

- *Multimedia* documents, including sound, music, image, and video files.

Learning About FTP by Reading the FAQ

An excellent way to learn more about any of the tools or resources on the Internet is to locate the frequently asked questions list for the topic in question.

By performing a simple Web search on the keywords **FAQ FTP**, I located a page with the FAQ question-and-answer list. At the top of the FAQ is a table of contents of all questions included on the list.

Finding FTP Documents at Large Archives

An excellent starting point for investigating FTP sites of interest is found in comprehensive listings maintained on Web pages. In the index illustrated in Figure 6.11, note the variety of subject categories of FTP documents included. FTP resource types available through this Web page include educational programs and materials, and graphics file archives containing drawings, artwork, and photographs. Also stored are multimedia documents and resources, as well as Usenet newsgroup archives and FAQs.

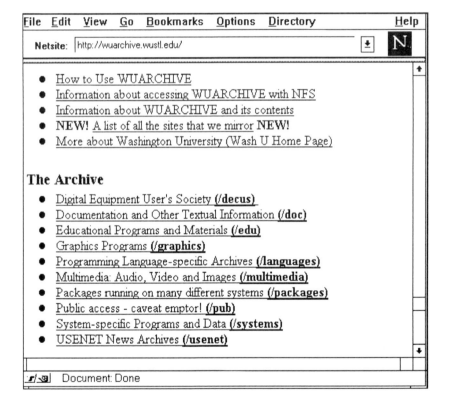

Fig. 6.11 An FTP archive site index on a Web page

http://www.luminet.net/~jackp/success.htm#fig6-11

Downloading Shareware at FTP Archive Sites

Software of various types can be freely downloaded from a large number of FTP sites on the Internet. As shown in Figure 6.12, I used a shareware FTP client program to access a large software archive at the site **ftp.coast.net**, which existed when this text was written. The rightmost window lists the files in the current directory at the remote FTP computer site I connected with (/mirrors/SimTel/win3). The window on the left displays the files on the local computer (note that I am currently in the c:\slip\cuteftp\ directory).

Changing directories with a Web browser or modern FTP client program running in a windowed environment is as simple as selecting the file or directory of your choice and clicking the mouse.

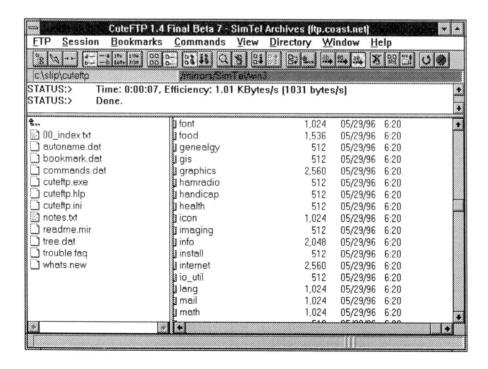

Fig. 6.12 A shareware FTP archive available on a Web page

Changing Directories at the FTP Site

Directories at FTP sites are arranged in a treelike fashion starting with the *root directory,* which is the main access point in the file system. From the root directory, you can move to a subdirectory using the **cd** (change directory) command. Using a Web browser or a more modern FTP client tool, however, allows the changing of directories to be accomplished by simply clicking the mouse on the directory or file of interest (behind the scenes, the program is sending the **cd** command to the FTP server for you). In Figure 6.13, we are currently in the /mirrors/simtelnet/win3/ directory at the ftp.coast.net site. Switching to the music subdirectory is performed using the **cd music** command in an older FTP (text-based) client program. (Note that file creation dates, times, and sizes in bytes are listed to the right of each directory or document.)

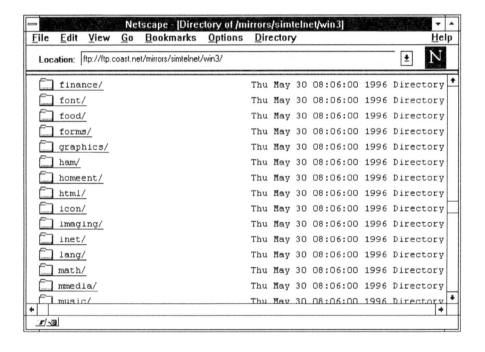

Fig. 6.13 Navigating the directory tree at an FTP site

Reading the Documentation Files at FTP Sites

After switching to the directory of your choice at an FTP site, a file is frequently included which lists information and more details about the various documents located there. In Figure 6.14, we have switched to the /mirrors/simtelnet/win3/music/ directory at the ftp.coast.net site, and a number of files are listed relating to music. Note the 00_index.txt file located at the top of the list, which is described on the following page.

While you are visiting an FTP site, it's valuable to take some time to read the index.txt, readme.txt, or similarly named files, since they provide useful information about the documents contained in that directory. If you're using a Web browser to view the contents of a text file at an FTP site, just click your mouse on the file of interest.

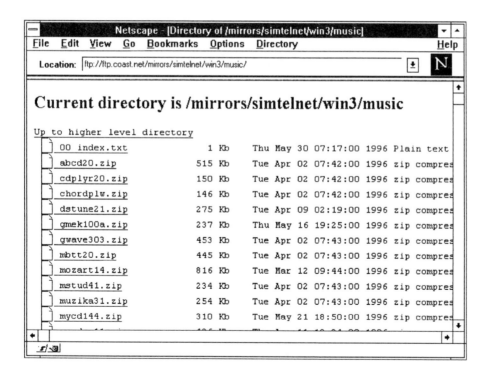

Fig. 6.14 A listing of music-related files on an FTP site

File Compression at FTP Sites

The contents of an index file are illustrated in Figure 6.15. Since space is always at a premium when storing computer files on FTP servers (and since larger files may take longer to download than smaller ones), files are often "compressed" to a more compact size when they are placed on an FTP site. *Compression* is a software scheme for crunching the information contained in a document to a significantly reduced size. Files ending with .z or .zip can be assumed to be in compressed form. After you download a compressed file to your site, you need to run another computer program (a "decompressor") before you can access it. Other types of compressed files include "self-extracting archives." These files, after downloading, are automatically decompressed by running them locally. Files ending with .exe (PC) and .sea (Mac) are examples of compressed filename suffixes used on personal computers. As stated earlier, *be careful of viruses!*

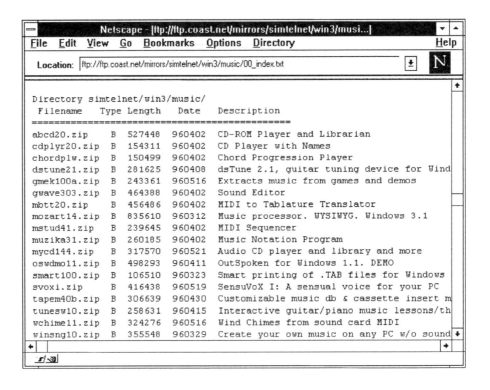

Fig. 6.15 Documentation of files in a subdirectory at an FTP site

Using a Decompression Program

After downloading the tunesw10.zip file from the FTP site depicted in Figure 6.15, I used a shareware utility program to decompress the file for use on my PC. (The Unzip shareware program used here was acquired from an anonymous FTP shareware archive on the Internet.)

Computer systems use differing compression schemes. Unix systems often compress files using filenames ending with .z, .gz, .zoo, or .tar, whereas DOS- and Windows-based PCs use .arc, .zip, or .zoo, and Macintosh computers use .sit or .hqx. (Decompressing Mac .sit files requires a program such as StuffIt for extracting the original files.) Using the PC-based Unzip decompression utility (Figure 6.16), I was required to enter the directory on my computer to store the decompressed files.

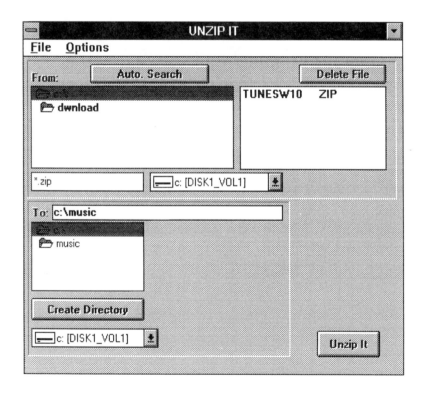

**Fig. 6.16 Using a shareware decompression
program after downloading**

Using Archie to Search for FTP Sites

It would be very cumbersome to find appropriate FTP sites if search engines, (such as Archie) were not available. Archie allows a user to search a large number of FTP archives for any files which relate to a topic of interest. Archie, like many Internet search engines, requests that you enter keyword(s) related to the subject you're investigating, and the engine will exhaustively canvass the Internet for anonymous FTP sites which match the topics you requested.

Archie can be accessed through Web pages and is accessible through many gopher sites (discussed in more detail later in this chapter).

6.4   Gopher Access to Internet Resources

Gopher is a user-friendly, menu-driven interface to the many different types of sites and resources available on the Internet. Gopher makes browsing the world of electronic information an effortless task. Gopher servers allow access to FTP sites and often include a link to the Archie search engine. Also, telnet sites can be accessed through gopher servers. Many colleges and universities throughout the world have developed gopher sites for presenting a CWIS (Campus Wide Information System) to the general public for disseminating information about their campuses.

The University of Minnesota Gopher Server

Since gopher was developed at the University of Minnesota, it's appropriate to include in our tour through "gopherspace" the U of M's "original" gopher site. An attractive feature of the gopher interface to the Internet is that all the information, tools, and resources are presented consistently—as a set of menu options on the display screen. Items which appear on the menus are clearly identified by a text description and an indicator denoting the *type* of resource listed. Gopher sites can also be accessed by modern Web browsers, where the menus are shown as pages (Figure 6.17). Clicking your mouse on any item listed will attempt to connect you to the resource—which is often another gopher menu displayed on a Web page.

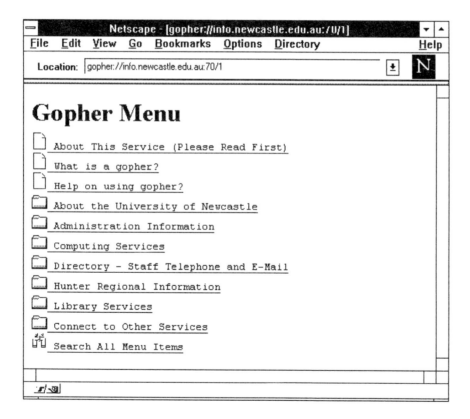

Fig. 6.17 University of Minnesota—birthplace of gopher

http://www.luminet.net/~jackp/success.htm#fig6-17

Popular FTP Sites Listed on a Gopher Server

Many gopher sites allow access to the Archie search engine which allows users to easily search for anonymous FTP sites in categories of interest. At the University of Minnesota gopher site illustrated in Figure 6.18, a menu includes an FTP sites option—which allows users to browse a list of "Popular FTP sites" (including archives for free software, gopher user documentation, Internet resource guides, and a huge variety of useful information in a wide breadth of different categories).

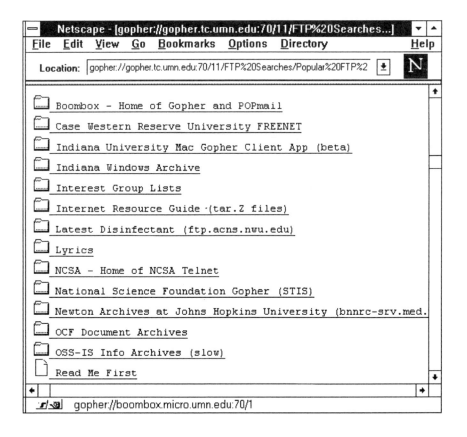

Fig. 6.18 Popular FTP sites listed on a gopher server

http://www.luminet.net/~jackp/success.htm#fig6-18

Choosing a Veronica Server for Searching Gopherspace

This text has emphasized the importance of using the searching facilities available when attempting to locate information on the Internet for a specific topic. A powerful searching engine for gopher sites has been developed named Veronica (note the relationship with Archie). Veronica is able to find gopher menus or documents on the Internet which match the areas requested by the user. The first step in using Veronica to find resources related to a topic of interest is to choose a server from the list shown at the menu of a typical gopher site. Sometimes you won't have luck reaching a server since it may be too busy or down at that time. Try again later, or choose a different server from the menu.

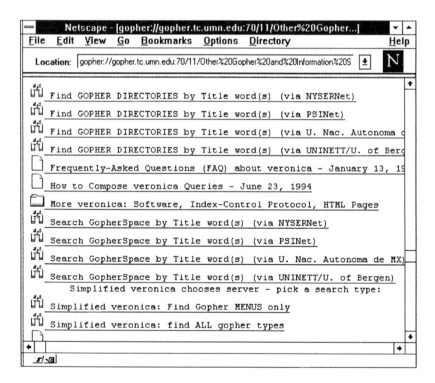

Fig. 6.19 A list of Veronica search engines at a gopher site

http://www.luminet.net/~jackp/success.htm#fig6-19

Searching Gopherspace with Veronica

In the previous menu, I chose the NYSERNet server, typing thoreau walden in the search form. I was led by a menu of "matches" to the screens shown in Figure 6.20.

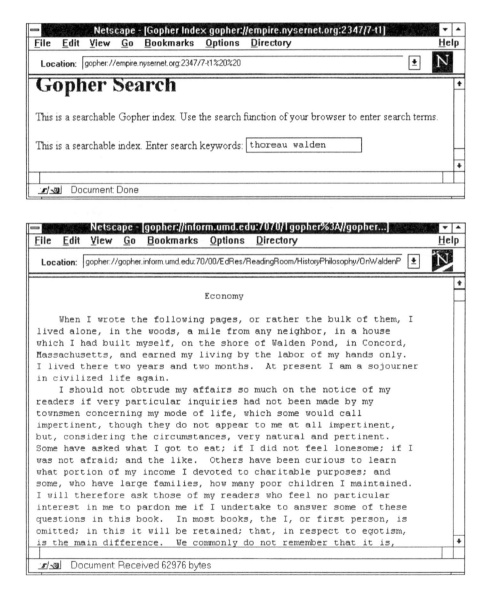

Fig. 6.20 Using Veronica to search for resources of interest via gopher

Becoming a Veronica "Guru" by Reading the FAQ

To find out more information about any Internet-related topic, locate the FAQ. For example, while writing this text, I needed to research some details on searching techniques using Veronica. By using a Web browser, I accessed a search engine to find gopher-related documents which included the words *information AND veronica*. I quickly located the gopher site shown in Figure 6.21 which had the Veronica FAQ I was looking for. FAQs are an excellent source of freely available information related to thousands of Internet-based resources.

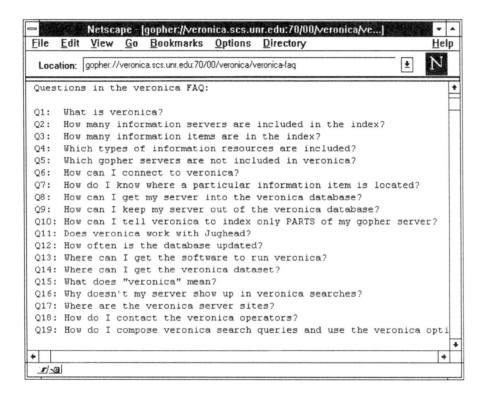

Fig. 6.21 The Veronica search engine FAQ at a gopher site

http://www.luminet.net/~jackp/success.htm#fig6-21

Gopher Access to Online Campus Publications

Gopher is a convenient medium for accessing a large variety of information useful to many college students. At the gopher site illustrated in Figure 6.22, the student has immediate access to online campus publications, including "electronic editions" of magazines and newspapers. Students worldwide are using sites on the Internet to display their works of poetry, art, literature, music, and many other areas of talent. Student-produced newspapers and electronic magazines (e-zines) can bring the educational community closer together and foster a sharing of ideas among students.

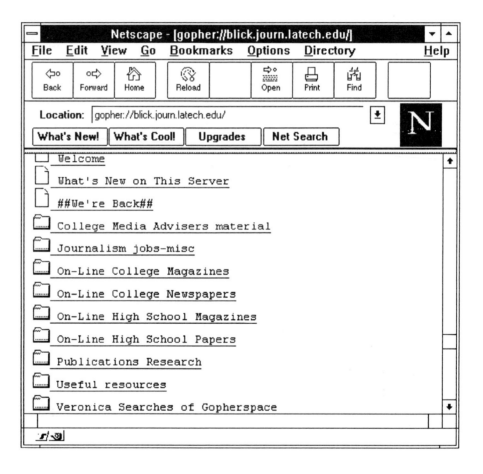

Fig. 6.22 A gopher site providing access to campus publications

http://www.luminet.net/~jackp/success.htm#fig6-22

Browsing Electronic Libraries with Gopher

Gopher sites throughout the world are repositories of large bodies of information on a variety of topics. Electronic virtual libraries of books and other publications are available in great abundance on the Internet. If you are researching a topic for a research paper or project, you may wish to try browsing the virtual libraries of the Internet through gopher. In Figure 6.23, a gopher menu at the University of Minnesota provides access to a large number of classic books and reference materials for students and other interested Internet surfers.

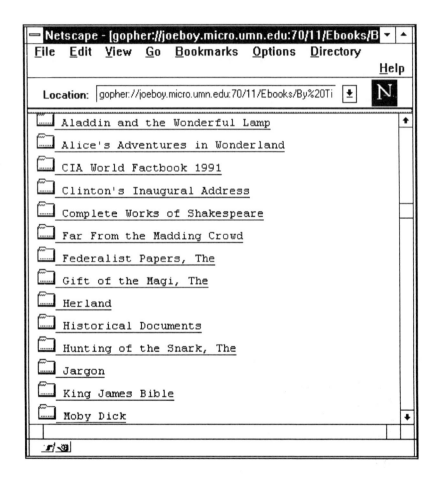

**Fig. 6.23 Books available in electronic
form through a gopher server**

http://www.luminet.net/~jackp/success.htm#fig6-23

6.5   Searching Electronic Databases Using WAIS

WAIS (wide-area information system) database access sites on the Internet allow users to look up information by keyword in large file and document archives stored in local or remotely located computer databases. Many educational institutions, libraries, research facilities, and organizations of all types have gathered large amounts of data which they have made available to the public. A WAIS server allows a database of computer files of any size or number to be easily searched by users who enter keywords related to the topic(s) of interest. Students can gain access to a tremendous volume of information in a large range of topics by accessing WAIS server computers on the Internet.

Searching NASA's Archives with WAIS

WAIS servers are powerful tools for searching large databases of documents which are maintained at computer sites on the Internet. WAIS allows the user to enter keyword(s) into the search engine; a list of documents which are "good matches" is returned (the document titles which best match the keywords entered by the user are placed near the top of the list).

Some variations of WAIS servers (such as *SWAIS*) allow you to enter "boolean operators" such as AND and OR, to specify the search criteria more specifically. For example, entering **Jupiter AND pictures** will perform a search for documents (in the SWAIS-accessed database) which contain both the words *Jupiter* and *pictures* (Figure 6.24).

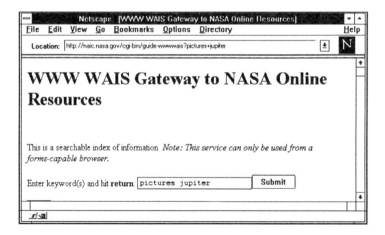

Fig. 6.24 Accessing WAIS servers through the Web

http://www.luminet.net/~jackp/success.htm#fig6-24

Searching for Sports Stats with WAIS

Information of all types can be found by browsing the databases using WAIS document searching engines. In the illustration shown in Figure 6.25, I performed a search on the keywords **sports statistics** and was shown a list of a number of sports-related documents available in databases from a particular WAIS site. (Some documents, unfortunately, were not an appropriate match to the subject I was researching.) Note that each document title scoring a "hit" by the WAIS engine is awarded a "matching score," which is a rough indication of the closeness to the desired match (a score of 1,000 designates a perfect match). As a convenience to the user, the type, size, and number of lines in each document is displayed along with each hit. Selecting the item on the WAIS search results screen links me directly to the document of interest.

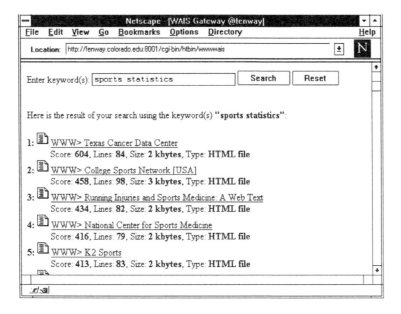

Fig. 6.25 Using WAIS to search sports-related Internet sites

Summary

Many different resource types exist on the Internet for use by students.

All sites on the Internet have a site name and an IP address associated with them.

Connecting to a server on the Internet requires a client program running on the user's computer or network or through remote telnet access.

All client programs first attempt to connect to the site requested by the user. Some programs perform the connection automatically on user request, and others require typing commands manually to the program.

Telnet allows a computer to be accessed remotely through the Internet.

Campus Wide Information Systems (CWISs) at colleges and universities frequently allow free telnet access to the public through the Internet.

When logged on to a remote computer using telnet, the user must follow the menus, screens, and commands at the host system.

Virus-infected documents are an imminent risk when downloading from unknown sources.

FTP allows a computer to transfer files through the Internet. An FTP site allows users to enter anonymously into its library of document archives, "snoop around" as desired, and retrieve (download) any files of interest.

Many large document archives of all types exist, including reference information; newsgroup FAQs; computer software, graphics and pictures, sounds, and other multimedia files; and data of various types.

During an FTP session, the user is in text or binary mode. Switching to binary mode with the **binary** command is recommended for transferring most file types.

Archie is a powerful "search by keyword" facility for locating FTP sites on the Internet. Archie can be reached through gopher servers, on the Web, and through Archie client programs.

Gopher is a very powerful Internet access facility which allows a student to locate and retrieve a large variety of resources in a very simple fashion by the use of menus and simple search screens.

Gopher sites typically provide a main menu which allows access to a rich variety of search engines, FTP sites, reference information, virtual libraries, CWIS sites, and access to information about the local system.

A gopher client program is needed to access a gopher site on the Internet. If gopher is not installed on your system, it is possible to use another institution's program by telnetting to its site. Modern Web browsers have the capability of acting as gopher clients.

Bookmarks of gopher sites may be kept by students to facilitate easy access at another time when they need to use a gopher site.

WAIS (wide-area information system) servers allow users to access volumes of data stored in databases on the Internet. Type in the keywords to the subject of interest, and WAIS will attempt to find any and all documents in the database which "match" your request.

A gateway to many WAIS servers is available on the World Wide Web. Using a Web browser to access WAIS database servers is convenient when those tools are available.

Web browsers can access most other site types, including WAIS databases, telnet sites, FTP servers, gopher sites (gopherspace), and mail servers.

Compression is a scheme for reducing the size of computer files. Smaller files mean less computer storage required and more rapid transfer times across the Internet.

It is often necessary to have a decompression utility (decompressor) at the local system to extract the original files from a downloaded archive file.

Review Questions

1. What is the principal purpose of telnet servers on the Internet?
2. Describe a reason for a CWIS being made available by a college or university to the public via the Internet.
3. What command is used in text-based telnet client programs to connect to a telnet server?
4. What is *HyTelnet,* and what is its purpose on the Internet?
5. Name a resource available at many telnet sites which would enable a student to find research articles in journals in an area of study.
6. List five resources useful for students that are available at anonymous FTP sites.

7. Define uploading and downloading as they relate to FTP.

8. What is usually entered as the password to gain access to an anonymous FTP site?

9. After logging onto a server, which FTP command prepares the system for downloading a word processing or graphics document?

10. Describe the difference between shareware and freeware.

11. State two reasons files are often archived in compressed form at anonymous FTP sites.

12. Describe the purpose of Archie and Veronica, and compare them.

13. How is information presented on a gopher site?

14. Describe two differences between gopher and the World Wide Web.

15. Describe the purpose of WAIS servers on the Internet and their value for students.

Credit Lines

Figure 4.3 Used by permission of CERN at the European Laboratory for Particle Physics.

Figure 4.6 Used by permission of The Weather Underground.

Figure 4.7 Reproduced with the permission of Digital Equipment Corporation. AltaVista and the AltaVista logo and the Digital logo are trademarks of Digital Equipment Corporation.

Figure 4.9 Text and artwork copyright © 1996 by YAHOO!, INC. All rights reserved. YAHOO! and the YAHOO! logo are trademarks of YAHOO!, Inc.

Figure 4.10 Reprinted by permission of Sally Murray and Roberta Barclay at the University of South Alabama Biomedical Library.

Figure 4.11 Used by permission of FinAid, Inc.

Figure 4.12 Used by permission of FinAid, Inc.

Figure 4.13 Used by permission of Greg Davis.

Figure 4.14 Reprinted by permission of the University of Oregon. Copyright 1996.

Figure 4.15 Used by permission of Honolulu Community College.

Figure 4.16 Used by permission of Honolulu Community College.

Figure 4.17 Used by permission of Rob Spragg, Coordinator of Library Web Services, University of Houston Libraries.

Figure 4.18 Used by permission of Paola Valladolid, Moderator of Digital Guitar Digest.

Figure 4.19 Used by permission of Miles Yoshimura.

Figure 4.20 Used by permission of the duPont-Ball Library, Stetson University.

Figure 4.21 By permission of GMI Engineering and Management Institute.

Figure 4.22 Used by permission.

Figure 4.23 Used by permission of the World Lecture Hall at the University of Texas, Austin.

Figure 4.24 Used by permission of WWWomen.

Figure 4.25 Used by permission of Maricopia Community College.

Figure 4.26 Used by permission of OCC.

Figure 4.27 Used by permission of OCC.

Figure 4.28 Used by permission of OCC.

Figure 6.4 Used by permission.

Figure 6.8 Used by permission.

Figure 6.11 Used by permission of the Office of the Network Coordinator, Washington University.

Figure 6.17 Used by permission of FormsNirvana Engineering, the University of Minnesota.

Figure 6.19 Used by permission of FormsNirvana Engineering, the University of Minnesota.

Figure 6.21 Copyright © Steven Foster 1993, 1994, 1995. This FAQ may be freely copied and redistributed provided it is copied entire and unmodified and this copyright statement remains intact. Reprinted by permission.

Figure 6.22 Used by permission of Eddie Blick, Louisiana Tech University.

Figure 6.24 Used by permission of M.I.T. AI Lab

Netscape Communications Corporation has not authorized, sponsored, or endorsed, or approved this publication and is not responsible for its content. Netscape and the Netscape Communications Corporate Logos, are trademarks and trade names of Netscape Communications Corporation. All other product names and/or logos are trademarks of their respective owners.

Index